# MEDIATION FOR LAWYERS

# Mediation for Lawyers

A PRACTICAL GUIDE FOR EFFECTIVE REPRESENTATION OF YOUR CLIENTS

*Suzanne Handman*

IRWIN LAW

Mediation for Lawyers


Published in 2024 by

Irwin Law Inc
Suite 206, 14 Duncan Street
Toronto, Ontario M5H 3G8
www.irwinlaw.com

ISBN: 978-1-55221-723-8 | e-book ISBN: 978-1-55221-724-5

**Cataloguing in Publication available from Library and Archives Canada**

Printed and bound by CPI Group (UK) Ltd, Croydon, CR0 4YY

1 2 3 4 5 27 26 25 24 23

*To my husband, Bjørn U. Ellingsen*
*My life partner and my rock*

# Summary Table of Contents

# Detailed Table of Contents

CHAPTER FIVE

## The Mediation Process 123

# Acknowledgements

I would like to thank several people for their input into this publication.

I am particularly indebted to my niece Wren Handman for her confidence in the value of my manuscript, her invaluable editing advice, and her suggestions to make the book a better read.

I am grateful to Me Robin Schiller for her careful review of my manuscript and for making pertinent comments to improve the text. I thank Me Jenna De Santis for having taken the time to read my manuscript and Me Murielle Korngold Wexler for reading my proposal. Their positive reaction to my project is appreciated. Renée Pellerin's experience as an author was most useful to me and was a guide for my proposal.

To the publisher of Irwin Law, the editors, and those who worked to typeset and proofread this book, I owe my gratitude for making my text a reality and bringing it to publication.

Finally, this book would not have been possible without the ongoing support of my husband, Bjørn U. Ellingsen, who read many parts of my drafts and provided useful feedback, encouragement, and assistance.

*chapter one*

# Introduction

## A. CHANGED ROLE OF LITIGATION LAWYERS

On my first day on the Bench in a labour tribunal, I quickly reviewed the proceedings and then noted that one of the parties had presented a motion. It was based on a provision in the *Civil Code*, requesting that the court refuse to allow the opposing party's expert witness testify at the trial. I was taken aback. I was sitting in a labour court and had only practiced labour law at the time. I was not familiar with the provision that was cited in the motion, and I had no time to learn about the issue raised before hearing the case.

I decided to meet the parties before the hearing, as often was the practice of the federal Labour Relations Board, where I had previously worked, adjudicating hearings. The lawyer, who had brought the expert to the Labour Tribunal, explained that this witness was a psychiatrist, and it was important that he testify. I was perplexed. I wondered what the reason was for a psychiatrist to be present at a hearing involving an employee who was suing his union for failing to represent him when he lost his job.

As I questioned the parties, the problem became clear. The employee in question had resigned from his position in the company, explaining that he was leaving to train for the Olympics. Several months later, he returned to his employer and asked for his job back. His employer agreed. After working for a short time, the employee resigned again, allegedly to train for the Olympics, and again returned to the company, requesting to be allowed to go back to work. The employer agreed for a second time. However, when the employee repeated his resignation for the third time and then requested to be reinstated in his position, his employer refused. In addition, the union refused to file a grievance on the employee's behalf.

This brought us to the question of the psychiatrist. Why was he present? At the time of the repeated resignations, the employee was suffering from a mental illness that caused grandiose ideas, leading him to believe he could compete in the Olympics, for which he was under treatment. At the time of the hearing, he had completed his treatment and, according to the psychiatrist, he was mentally well. There was no risk of him continuing to behave as he had done in the past.

With further questioning, I learned that the employee had been a good worker and the employer was satisfied with him. Once the employer heard from the psychiatrist that the employee was no longer delusional, the employer agreed to reinstate him.

However, the union raised the issue of the employee's seniority. If he returned to work, it would affect the seniority of other employees. After considerable discussion with all three parties and their respective lawyers, they reached a compromise with respect to the seniority status of this employee. There was then no need for a hearing.

My jurisdiction in such cases at this tribunal was limited. If I granted the employee's application, I would order the union to bring the employee's case before an arbitrator. I did not have the authority to grant the employee's reinstatement. By reaching an agreement, all the parties were satisfied. The employee got his job back and all the players involved in the case avoided another hearing. It was a win-win solution.

Clearly, finding a means of dispute resolution is a preferred way to deal with conflicts. It leads to a greater satisfaction for the parties than a trial.

This chapter deals with the means of preventing conflicts and of the methods that exist to resolve them. Some methods are better known than others. However, it is useful for counsel to be aware of all existing methods. In this way, the lawyer is in a better position to provide sound advice.

* * * * *

The role of a litigation lawyer has evolved over time. The traditional approach is well-known: An individual or group consults you about a lawsuit they wish to institute against another person, company, or organization, or they consult you because they have been sued. They most often feel aggrieved and have suffered material, physical, or moral damages, or any combination of such losses. The reasons leading them to seek legal counsel include any one of the myriad cases that come before the court.

You review the facts your clients have presented. You explain the applicable law. You consider that your clients have an excellent case. You are prepared to institute a lawsuit on their behalf, and you explain the various aspects of litigation, including the possibility of examinations before and after defence, of interlocutory proceedings, and, depending on the nature of the case, of requiring an expert report, as well as going over the potential duration of the trial, your hourly fee, other expenses, and so on.

If you represent the opposing party, you will provide them with the appropriate information about how you will defend them. You will deny the claim in your response to the other party's demand letter, and you will draft a defence. In both cases, whether you are representing the plaintiffs or the defendants, you will ultimately litigate the case in court.

In the past, suggesting to your clients that they settle their case was seen as a sign of weakness. Your clients would likely consider you to be incapable of representing them. Proposing a settlement to the opposite party was also considered a sign of weakness. Any attempt to settle was typically seen to imply that your clients did not have a good case either in fact or in law, or that they would not be credible witnesses. It could also have meant that you did not have sufficient or strong evidence to support their claim, including the lack of adequate expert witnesses, or be viewed as an indication that you were simply incapable of litigating the file or you were afraid of going to court.

The legal culture has changed. It is no longer considered to be a weakness to propose a means of settling a dispute to your own clients or to the opposite party, rather than litigating a conflict. In fact, our Canadian courts encourage parties to settle. Negotiation between lawyers is not a new method in attempting to resolve litigation amicably. However, recent approaches to resolving disputes include not only negotiation but also mediation, judicial settlement conferences, and other methods of participative justice.

Dispute resolution mechanisms have emerged over the past several decades. In all provinces and territories in Canada and in many other countries, this reality has been incorporated into the law. Legislation varies, however, from one jurisdiction to another and from one court to another. In some jurisdictions, prevention and resolution processes must be considered before referring a dispute to a court. In other locations, dispute resolution mechanisms are encouraged, while in others, such mechanisms are obligatory for certain types of cases, as stipulated in statutes, regulations, court rules, or judicial practice directions.

Since the legal culture has changed, it is important for you, as a lawyer, to be aware of the various dispute resolution mechanisms that exist and to be comfortable proposing such mechanisms to your clients and to the opposing party. It is also important to be comfortable in actively participating in and representing your clients in such processes.

The purpose of this book is to treat the changed role of litigation lawyers, dealing with your position as counsel in dispute resolution. There are various means available to resolve conflict. However, here the focus will be on interest-based mediation, whether it is private mediation or judicial mediation, as opposed to an evaluative mediation process.

Since the laws governing mediation and settlement conferences differ from one jurisdiction to another, this book does not attempt to deal with the legislation regarding settlement procedures in each individual jurisdiction. It is therefore necessary for you, the reader, to determine what rules apply in the location in which you practice. However, the classic interest-based mediation process is essentially the same across Canada, as well as in many other countries, and it is this method that the book will discuss.

This book is intended to be practical rather than theoretical. Its goal is to familiarize you, as a lawyer, with mediation as a mechanism, and to provide you with the necessary information so that you can represent your clients effectively, with assurance and ease, at every stage of the mediation process.

The number of references listed is limited. Some topics were inspired by books or articles on the subject, and in such instances the sources are acknowledged. However, for the most part, the role of a lawyer in initiating the mediation process, preparing for mediation, and participating in mediation sessions is based on my personal experience as a mediator, both in judicial settlement conferences and in private mediations.

When presiding over mediation sessions, I noticed the difference between those lawyers who were genuinely interested in helping their clients come to a settlement and those who were still trying to litigate the case during the mediation. Where the lawyers were intent on being of assistance, their clients appeared comfortable and assured. Very often, these lawyers were very instrumental in suggesting creative solutions that ultimately worked. Conversely, those who tried to maintain their traditional litigation role were not helpful. They tended to be aggressive and failed to collaborate. They put brakes on the process or caused unnecessary anxiety in their clients. Frequently, the difference in approach depended on whether the lawyers were familiar with the mediation process and felt capable of assisting their clients.

I noted that while lawyers always prepared for a trial, this was not the case for mediations or settlement conferences. I attribute this to the fact that many lawyers are simply not aware of how a mediation proceeds and how to prepare for it. This was evident in the many mediation sessions that I presided over. The lawyers would arrive, armed with heavy briefcases, planning to use their proceedings and exhibits for reference purposes. I always asked them to put their files away. The lawyers usually looked confused but followed my instructions.

When I began to explain the process, which begins with each party relating how they met each other and telling their version of the facts, the lawyers typically stated that they did not need to hear the parties' versions, since both parties were aware of what had taken place. They wanted to begin negotiating. This, however, is not how the process works. After the parties finished telling their stories, the lawyers tried to cross-examine them, as they would do in a trial. This is also not how the process works.

Finally, after the initial steps of the process were completed, I asked the parties to suggest a means of resolving their conflict, given the issues raised. The parties most often looked at me blankly. When I questioned the lawyers as to the discussions they had with their clients before coming to the mediation, they freely admitted they had not talked to them about what monetary solution or other means would be acceptable to resolve their conflict.

It was clear that the lawyers had not prepared for the mediation, nor had they prepared their clients to participate in the session. I surmised that, in all probability, they did not know how to do so. In other cases, the lawyers had experience with mediations but were not very effective in helping their clients.

This lack of familiarity with the settlement process by many lawyers or their lack of effectiveness led me to write this book. It is my hope that it will encourage more lawyers to participate in dispute resolution processes and that it will be beneficial for all those who are involved in settlement procedures, whether they are neophytes in mediation or have already had experience.

## B. PREVENTION AND DISPUTE RESOLUTION

The first term used to describe the various methods of resolving conflicts was alternative dispute resolution, commonly known as

ADR.[1] ADR dates from the late 1970s as a legal reform movement in the United States. At the outset, the term was coined to describe the resolution of disputes by a means other than by traditional litigation in the courts.

Over time, the term has evolved. While the acronym ADR and the term alternative dispute resolution are still used, some refer to the process as *appropriate* dispute resolution,[2] while others prefer *mechanisms for resolving disputes* or simply *dispute resolution*,[3] since these latter terms encompass all mechanisms that could be applied and are available for resolving conflict. Accordingly, these terms would include not only private extrajudicial means of bringing parties to settle, but also settlement conferences, presided over by a judge.

The expression used for the various tools has little importance. What is more important is that parties who participate in the process of resolving their conflict have the same understanding of what is involved when they refer to a particular dispute mechanism.

The means used to deal with disputes range from preventing a conflict from taking place to facilitating a decision rendered by a quasi-judicial tribunal or a judgment rendered by a court. Given that this text deals with mediation as a dispute resolution method, other means of resolving conflict will be described only in a summary fashion primarily to ensure that, in suggesting mediation to your clients, you are able not only to describe this method, but the other methods that exist as well.

Knowledge of the basic elements involved in each of the different methods will also provide you with the ability to explain the reason for choosing mediation, if this is the method you recommend.

---

1 Carrie Menkel-Meadow, "The History and Development of 'A'DR (Alternative/Appropriate Dispute Resolution)" (1 July 2016), online: https://voelkerrechtsblog.org/de/the-history-and-development-of-a-dr-alternativeappropriate-dispute-resolution.

2 *Ibid* at para 2.

3 Resolution Systems Institute, "Court ADR Basics: Overview," online: www.aboutrsi.org/resource-center/court-adr-basics; Government of Canada, "Resolving Disputes — Think About Your Options" (25 August 2022), online: www.justice.gc.ca/eng/rp-pr/csj-sjc/dprs-sprd/dr-rd/index.html.

Obviously, the best way to avoid a conflict is to prevent it from taking place. Most often, a dispute can be averted by a simple consultation with a lawyer. However, misunderstandings and disputes do occur, and when they do, several different methods exist for resolving them, as outlined below.

### 1) Prevention

The methods for preventing conflict include the following:

#### a) Consultation with a Lawyer

It is always preferable to prevent conflict instead of trying to resolve it afterwards. Consulting a lawyer for any situation that could have legal implications, while not a guarantee that conflict will never occur, is the most appropriate approach to take.

A consultation will allow clients to be aware of their rights and obligations. It will provide them with information to determine beforehand whether a decision they wish to take is legal, or what consequences, if any, can result from a particular course of action. In this way, clients can make decisions with full knowledge of any legal implications that can potentially follow.

If you are involved in drafting any legal documents for clients, whether a partnership agreement, a sales contract, a commercial lease, an employment contract, a franchise agreement, or any other matter, consider recommending the inclusion of a clause stipulating that if a conflict arises in the interpretation or application of the agreement, the parties undertake to deal with the conflict by means of mediation or another form of dispute resolution.

The following is an example of such a contract requiring the parties to resort to mediation in the event of a dispute.

The parties to this contract agree that:

- Any dispute that may arise regarding the interpretation, performance, or enforcement of this contract or agreement will, before resorting to litigation, be submitted to mediation.
- Either party may send a written notice to mediate to the other party and shall specify the issues in dispute.

- The parties will jointly select a mediator from the list of certified mediators (of the ________ Bar association or the Dispute Resolution organization of ______) within __ days from the date of notice.
- The mediation shall be held within __ days after a mediator has been selected.
- The mediation shall take place at ______ (or the mediation will be held virtually by means of the following platform: _________).
- The parties agree to exchange any information which they intend to rely upon during the mediation at least ___ days before the mediation session.
- The parties will participate in the mediation process in good faith and attempt to resolve their dispute in an amiable manner.
- The costs of the mediation, including any fees and expenses of the mediator, shall be shared equally by the parties.
- All discussions held before, during, or after the mediation, as well as documents used or exchanged by the parties which are not part of the court record and which cannot otherwise be legally introduced into evidence, are confidential and cannot be divulged under any circumstances (or can only be divulged to establish the existence or terms of the settlement).
- The results of any agreement reached in mediation shall be final and binding on the parties, without appeal.

Additional clauses can be considered, such as the selection of the presiding mediator from a specified list on a rotating basis, the right of the mediator to meet with each party separately, if that is deemed to be appropriate, the obligation of the mediator and other participants to maintain the confidentiality of all aspects of the mediation process, the voluntary nature of the process, and the ability of the parties to terminate the mediation at any time, and so on. More detailed clauses dealing with the confidential aspect of the process will be found under the heading *Confidentiality Agreement* in Chapter 2, Section H.

### b) Facilitation

Facilitation is considered as a means of preventing conflict. It is used prior to a conflict arising. In this process, a neutral person, namely the facilitator, helps a public or private group, whether small or large, work together more effectively and in a more collaborative way to reach a consensus, a solution, or a common goal, and to avoid any conflict in so doing.

Facilitations can involve a one-time meeting or many meetings. In the latter case, the meetings can continue over an extended period, for as long as necessary to accomplish the result the group is looking for.

Facilitators may be part of the organization or external to it. Their role is to plan, guide, and lead the group process by overseeing the organization, its agenda, and its progress, and bring the project to a successful conclusion.

Facilitators assist those involved to be more focused and efficient. They help improve the way in which the clients communicate with each other, cooperate, solve problems, and reach decisions. Facilitators have no authority to make decisions.[4]

As opposed to mediation, where the goal is to reach an agreement, the goal in facilitation is to help the group achieve what they set out to do—for example, creating an action plan for a given organization or a vision statement, planning for an underprivileged area of a city, preparing recommendations for decision-making, and so on. The process and the agenda are determined by the group. The decisions are reached by a decision-making process that is decided by the group, in contrast to mediation, which involves a process that is determined by the mediator.[5]

Facilitation can be extremely useful in providing a forum for clarifying misunderstandings, avoiding conflict, and helping

---

4 Brad Spangler, "Facilitation" in Guy Burgess & Heidi Burgess, eds, *Beyond Intractability*, University of Colorado Conflict Information Consortium (July 2003), online: www.beyondintractability.org/essay/facilitation.

5 Janice M. Fleischer & Zena D. Zumeta, "Preventing Conflict through Facilitation" *Mediate* (23 December 1999), online: https://mediate.com/preventing-conflict-through-facilitation.

groups develop a consensus on issues of concern to them. However, once conflict arises, more appropriate methods exist, as outlined below.

## 2) Dispute Resolution

There is a continuum in the means of dealing with conflict that can run from negotiation to a trial. As the method moves toward a decision-making process, it becomes more formal, more complex, costlier, and less timely. In addition, the impartial third party, who presides over the process, plays a more active and central role, and in the case of a trial, ultimately decides the outcome of the conflict.

### a) Negotiation

Negotiation has been defined as any form of communication where the parties, having opposing interests, discuss the joint action they can take to deal with a dispute between them.[6] It is also referred to as a decision-making process where two or more parties, having different preferences, need to reach a joint decision.[7] It is essentially a method which may be competitive or collaborative, and where there is a willingness on the part of the parties to settle an existing conflict[8] or agree to an outcome that is mutually satisfactory.

Negotiation consists of informal meetings or discussions between two or more parties. It can be used not only to resolve an existing issue in a way both parties find acceptable, but also to modify their relations and create the basis for a future relationship.

---

6 Government of Canada, "Negotiation" *Dispute Resolution Reference Guide* (25 August 2022), online: www.justice.gc.ca/eng/rp-pr/csj-sjc/dprs-sprd/res/drrg-mrrc/03.html.

7 Katie Shonk, "What is Negotiation?" Program on Negotiation, Harvard Law School Daily Blog (23 March 2023), online: www.pon.harvard.edu/daily/negotiation-skills-daily/what-is-negotiation.

8 M^e^ Jean-Yves Brière, "Compléter le plan d'une négociation" (2023–24) *Collection des Habiletés, Justice Participative*, Barreau du Québec 53 at 54.

The process is voluntary, non-adjudicative, and flexible. The parties may negotiate publicly or privately. However, the process is generally confidential. It is the parties themselves who are involved, although they may be represented by an attorney, a friend, or another professional. In contrast to negotiations that take place within mediation, or other methods of dispute resolution, there is no intervention by a neutral third party.[9]

One of the advantages of negotiation is in procedural terms. Negotiation is the most flexible form of dispute resolution, since it only involves the parties who have an interest in the matter or their representatives, if any. The parties can shape the negotiations according to their needs and design an agreement which reflects their interests. However, the absence of a neutral third party may be a disadvantage, particularly in situations of unequal power. The parties may be unable to reach an agreement without the intervention and help of a neutral third party.

Traditionally, each party sets out their respective position, and tries to persuade the other to accept it, seeking to achieve the best possible outcome. During their exchanges, the parties communicate their rights and objectives to each other. This style is labelled as competitive bargaining or positional based negotiation, its focus being on specific positions.

It should be noted that authors Fisher and Ury in their well-known text, *Getting to Yes: Negotiating Agreement Without Giving In*,[10] state that rather than bargaining with the focus on their individual positions, the parties can achieve a wise agreement with an amicable outcome by means of a method that permits a consensus on a joint decision. This principled method focuses on using basic interests, mutually satisfying options, and fair standards.

In such cooperative negotiations, one party's gains are not necessarily achieved at the other party's expense. This form of cooperative or collaborative negotiating style, also known as

---

9 Government of Canada, "Negotiation," above note 6.

10 Roger Fisher & William Ury, *Getting to Yes: Negotiating Agreement Without Giving In*, rev ed (New York, NY: Penguin Books, 2011) at 1–15.

principled negotiation or principled bargaining, has gained wide acceptance and increasing use.[11] Collaborative negotiations will be discussed in more detail in Chapter 5.

### b) Mediation

Mediation is one of the most frequently used dispute resolution processes. In mediation, a neutral and impartial third party, the mediator, intervenes to assist the parties in resolving their dispute.

Mediators, using communication techniques, help the parties to identify the issues to be resolved and to communicate their different perspectives more effectively. Mediators explore the interests and needs of the parties, assist the parties in negotiating with each other and in selecting options for settlement, and seek ways to help them resolve their conflict in a mutually acceptable way.[12]

Mediators control the process and are proactive with respect to its content. In the classic approach, mediators have no authority to render a decision, impose an agreement, or even determine the outcome of the conflict. Their role is to help the parties find their own solution, and one that is satisfactory to them.

Contrary to this method, when the parties seek an approach of evaluative mediation, mediators are hired to provide an opinion on the outcome of the conflict. Generally, mediators encourage the parties to accept their proposition for settlement.

Accordingly, the approach of the mediator can vary. The different mediation models include classic or facilitative mediation, evaluative mediation, and transformative mediation. The differences with respect to the two principal methods—namely, the classic approach and evaluative mediation—will be outlined in more detail in a later section.

The advantages of mediation are numerous, the most important being the possibility of finding a solution to the conflict that meets the parties' interests and needs. Parties often opt to resolve

11 Government of Canada, "Negotiation," above note 6.

12 The articles written on mediation are too numerous to list. The content regarding mediation is based primarily on the author's experience and on courses given by the author.

their case by means of mediation because of the confidential nature of the process, as well as to avoid the time delays, stress, and expense of a trial. A detailed list of the advantages will be provided in a later section.

The disadvantages of mediation are few. The process may be problematic in cases of a power imbalance between the parties without strategies to mitigate this situation. In addition, parties can use mediation as a *fishing expedition* without the intention of reaching an agreement.

In most jurisdictions, the process is voluntary. Even where mediation is mandatory and the parties are required to participate in a mediation session, they are not required to resolve their conflict, and the mediator is not empowered to impose a decision.

Lawyers play an important role in mediation. They explain the nature of the process; contact the opposing party or lawyer to determine whether they agree to participate in a mediation; advise their clients with respect to the choice of a mediator; prepare their clients for the mediation session(s); participate in the process by assisting their clients to communicate appropriately; negotiate; select options; and conclude an agreement. Ultimately, lawyers protect their clients' interests and provide advice throughout the process.

The initiation of the mediation process, the preparation for mediation, and the mediation process itself will be dealt with extensively in later sections.

### c) Early Neutral Evaluation

Early neutral evaluation, or neutral evaluation, is a process in which the parties, or their lawyers, present their case to a knowledgeable, competent, and experienced neutral evaluator or third party, generally a lawyer, who is a highly respected specialist in the field of the dispute.[13]

---

13 Government of Canada, "Neutral Evaluation" *Dispute Resolution Reference Guide* (25 August 2022), online: www.justice.gc.ca/eng/rp-pr/csj-sjc/dprs-sprd/res/drrg-mrrc/eval.html; FindLaw, "Neutral Evaluation: An ADR Technique Whose

When the problem is complicated or technical in nature, the parties may select a neutral evaluator who is not an attorney but who is an expert in the concerned field. Such a person would readily be able to grasp the complex issues involved.

Early neutral evaluation can be initiated at any time during a conflict, but an assessment of the case early in the process is preferable. The parties present a concise written "evaluation statement" of the issue, including the facts, expert reports, the law, arguments, and judicial cases. Each party at the session presents an oral summary of the factual and legal basis of their position.

Neutral evaluators assess the strengths and weaknesses of each side's case, in fact, law, or both. They then give the parties an opinion regarding the likely conclusions that a judge or an arbitrator would reach following a trial or an arbitration hearing. A neutral evaluator's evaluation with respect to the merits of the case is not binding on the parties. That said, the evaluation may nevertheless assist the parties in negotiating with improved understanding.

This process, which is voluntary, informal, flexible, and usually confidential, is similar to a mini trial, but more affordable. The main purpose of early neutral evaluation is to reduce litigation costs by encouraging open communication between the parties and providing them with an expert's early and realistic assessment of the case before unnecessary costs and delays ensue.

The role of the neutral third party, in addition to helping the parties identify the issues in dispute, assessing the strengths and weaknesses of their cases, and providing an opinion as to the probable outcome of the case in court, involves introducing the parties to a new perspective. Neutral evaluators help each of the parties understand the other's stance. They try to find common ground and explore the possibility of discussing a settlement. If the parties agree, neutral evaluators can choose any format acceptable to the parties, including assuming the role of a mediator.

---

Time Has Come" (24 January 2017), online: https://corporate.findlaw.com/litigation-disputes/neutral-evaluation-an-adr-technique-whose-time-has-come.html.

The assessment provided by early neutral evaluation helps the parties recognize any limitations in their case and favours a prompt, early settlement. It is particularly useful where parties either need to maintain an ongoing relationship or are interested in doing so. It allows them to avoid litigation that can render a continued relationship improbable. While there are many advantages to early neutral evaluation, it may be vulnerable to manipulation when used as a delay tactic, to preview the case of the opposing party, or when pursued in bad faith.

The presence of a lawyer is advisable. Lawyers are instrumental in deciding whether to opt for this mechanism. If they do choose this method, they determine when the process will take place and aid in the selection of the neutral third party. They also have the role of determining the issues to be presented, of presenting written and oral submissions on behalf of their clients, and, should settlement discussions take place, of assisting their clients in negotiating the most beneficial result possible.

### d) The Mini Trial

The mini trial has been described as a structured negotiated settlement technique that is designed in a manner similar to an expedited trial. It provides a means for the parties to hear the other side's point of view and attempt a negotiated settlement, often allowing them to achieve practical solutions that are rarely gained through the adversarial litigation process.[14]

In essence, the mini trial is a non-judicial, expedited, voluntary, confidential, informal, and non-binding procedure, used primarily in the context of commercial conflicts[15] that present complex questions of fact and law. It can, for example, be used to settle

14 Government of Canada, "The Mini-Trial" *Dispute Resolution Reference Guide* (25 August 2022), online: www.justice.gc.ca/eng/rp-pr/csj-sjc/dprs-sprd/res/drrg-mrrc/05.html.

15 Bob Frie, Jim Arndt & Paul Danborn, "Alternative Dispute Resolution — Mini Trial" (2023), online: https://friearndt.com/mediationarbitration/alternative-dispute-resolution-mini-trial.

conflicts related to non-compete issues, patents and trademarks, product liability, and so on.

The process is carried out before a panel composed of a senior representative of each company involved (as, for example, the director general or a senior corporate manager) who have the authority to negotiate a settlement. The panel is chaired by a neutral, independent person jointly selected by the parties who has their respect and confidence.

The role of the neutral third person varies. It may be limited to facilitating communication and ensuring rules of procedure, or it may be enlarged to include issuing a non-binding opinion as to the possible outcome of a case, recommending a specific outcome, or acting as a mediator during subsequent negotiations.

The parties are represented by legal counsel, who provide the neutral chairperson with legal briefs and can present evidence and arguments according to the rules established in the mini trial agreement. After the presentation by both lawyers, the management representatives meet by themselves and try to see if they can settle the dispute.

If the representatives are unable to settle on their own, they can ask the neutral third person to provide them with an oral or written opinion on the issues and the likely outcome at a trial. Alternatively, the representatives can ask the neutral panel member to mediate and help bring the case to a resolution.[16] The means of resolving the conflict are usually more of a business nature than a legal one.

The mini trial is less costly than litigation and causes less of a business disruption between the parties. However, the trial-like nature of the hearing may continue to polarize the positions of the parties rather than promoting an atmosphere of cooperation. In addition, the expense may be wasted if the parties could have resolved the conflict through negotiations or mediation.

---

16 *West's Encyclopedia of American Law*, 2d ed, "Minitrial," online: https://legal-dictionary.thefreedictionary.com/Minitrial.

The lawyers' role is akin to their role in litigation—namely, they will handle examinations, prepare briefs or position papers, and present their clients' cases before the panel. If the parties settle, the lawyers also play a role in drafting the mini trial settlement agreement. However, unlike the conciliatory or settlement-oriented role played by lawyers in other dispute resolution procedures, in this procedure, the representatives of the companies involved are responsible for negotiating a settlement, not the lawyers.

#### e) Arbitration

Arbitration, a well-known process, is another means of settling disputes. In this method, the parties jointly choose to submit an actual or eventual conflict to the decision of one or more arbitrators, who alone or with others constitute the arbitration tribunal. In the case of a tripartite tribunal, each party selects a representative who participates with the presiding arbitrator.

The arbitrator, who presides over the hearing, is neutral and independent. Conventional arbitration can be a private, ad hoc mechanism that is generally specialized in a particular area of endeavour and whose authority stems from a private arbitration agreement.[17] Arbitration may also be required by statute as a means of resolving disputes, as in the case of labour conflicts in a unionized setting.

Arbitration is an adversarial process in nature. The parties provide the tribunal with a statement of their positions and their exhibits. A hearing is held, in which witnesses are heard and arguments are presented. Following the hearing, the tribunal renders a decision, which is final—there is no appeal.

In sum, the arbitration tribunal is called upon by the parties to decide a conflict, in the same way a judge handles a case in trial. However, the procedure is simpler and less formal than before the courts. It is conducted in private and may be confidential. Decisions are obtained more rapidly, and at a lower cost than trials.

---

17 Olivier Després, "L'arbitrage conventionnel" (2023–24), *Collection des Habiletés, Justice Participative*, Barreau du Québec at 105–7.

However, in the case of an arbitration tribunal composed of three members, the costs may be significantly higher than when a single arbitrator hears a case.

The arbitration award may be binding or non-binding,[18] depending on whether the procedure is determined by law, or by agreement pursuant to an arbitration clause in a contract. In the case of binding arbitration, the arbitration award can be enforced, giving the award the same effect as a court judgment.

Parties often opt for arbitration because of its capacity to resolve disputes quickly. It also provides the disputants with the opportunity to choose the arbitrator who will decide the issues in question and often has expertise in the subject matter. The rules of procedure may be as formal or informal as the parties determine, and the costs can be more easily contained. However, awards have no precedential value, and recourse against an award is extremely limited.

Arbitration is the required means of dealing with conflict in labour relations. It is widely used in commercial disputes as a private alternative to litigation, and it may be used in civil conflicts as well. Parties are generally represented by attorneys, whose role is similar to that which they assume in court.

### f) Med/Arb

Med/arb is a process that consists of a combination of both mediation and arbitration. The neutral third party is mandated by the parties to act initially as a mediator. If the parties are unable to resolve all the issues in their dispute through the mediation process, the neutral third party assumes the role of arbitrator and

18 Government of Canada, "Arbitration" *Dispute Resolution Reference Guide* (25 August 2022), online: www.justice.gc.ca/eng/rp-pr/csj-sjc/dprs-sprd/res/drrg-mrrc/06.html. Labour legislation foresees that arbitration awards are binding. Legislation governing other matters may also stipulate that arbitration awards are binding on the parties. However, where the arbitration is held in accordance with a contract concluded by the parties, nothing prevents them from clearly specifying in the arbitration clause of their contract that the decision is not binding, according to agreed upon modalities.

renders a decision on the conflict as a whole or on any outstanding issues.[19]

One of the advantages of such a process is that parties who opt for a med/arb process have the certainty of either concluding an agreement or obtaining a decision at the end of the process. In fact, many parties want to hear mediators express their opinion on how they should settle their dispute, rather than have the mediators help the parties find their own solution.

There has been criticism of this hybrid process. Because the mediator-arbitrator will render a decision if the parties are unable to reach an agreement, the parties may be reluctant to divulge certain information, which could be relevant in bringing about a settlement. The unwillingness or the failure to be open negatively impacts on the mediation process.

In addition, parties who believe they have a stronger case than their opponent may be more reluctant to settle their conflict in the hope that their position will prevail at the arbitration stage. Since the mediator can hold caucuses and meet separately with each of the parties, the mediator may obtain information on a confidential basis, which could potentially influence the decision to the detriment of the other party.

Despite the drawbacks described above, this method is used in civil, commercial, and labour relations cases.

### g) Arb/Med

Another hybrid process is arb/med. This is a process similar to med/arb, the difference being that the parties begin with an arbitration proceeding which results in the issuance of a non-binding award. Then the parties work with a mediator in their attempt to resolve their conflict.

This process is less common than med/arb. One of the problems is that beginning with a confrontational process is not very favourable to a subsequent process of having parties approach each other in a collaborative way during the mediation process.

---

19 Miville Tremblay, "La Justice Participative" (2023–24), *Collection des Habiletés, Justice Participative*, Barreau du Québec 7 at 21–22

### h) Judicial Mediation or Settlement Conferences

Judicial mediation, which is also called a settlement conference, is a means of dispute resolution, presided by judges or adjudicators, which provides litigants with an alternate forum of access to justice.

The objective of a settlement conference is to resolve the conflict so that a trial will either be unnecessary or, at most, limited to those issues on which the parties do not agree. The process is aimed at helping parties communicate and better understand their respective needs, interests, and positions, and ultimately reach a mutually satisfactory agreement to resolve their conflict.

The meeting takes place in an institutional setting, namely the courthouse or a tribunal. With few exceptions, the judge-mediator is selected by the court or tribunal and is not remunerated by the parties. However, in Alberta, lawyers are permitted to select the judge they want to conduct their settlement conference, which is known as Judicial Dispute Resolution (JDR).[20]

Given the fact that judge/mediators exercise their role within an institutional context, they have less flexibility in adapting their approach to the needs or desires of the parties. While the objective of the process is the same as private mediation, judges, because of their position and moral authority, may be instrumental in bringing about settlements more easily than in private mediation.

As outlined in a later section, depending on the jurisdiction in which judges exercise their functions, there is a difference as to the role a judge plays in dispute resolution. In most jurisdictions where judicial mediation is available, the judge acts as a neutral party and assists the parties in their attempt to reach an agreement but does not decide the outcome. However, in other jurisdictions,

---

20 Justice Robert A. Graesser, "Judicial Dispute Resolution, Alberta Style" *Canadian Institute for the Administration of Justice* (2016), online: (PDF) https://ciaj-icaj.ca/wp-content/uploads/documents/2016/05/m5.pdf?id=7733&1659726385. Counsel can send their choice of judge to the court trial coordinators, who schedule the JDR sessions.

the judge has the role of evaluating a case and issuing a binding decision on its merits.[21]

The role of lawyers also varies depending on the jurisdiction in which they practice. In the context of a process that does not involve a judge's evaluation, attorneys must prepare their clients to participate in the judicial mediation session or settlement conference as they would for a traditional mediation session. During the process, lawyers assume an advisory role.

In a process where judges provide their assessment of the parties' strengths and weaknesses and advise the parties as to the ruling another judge would make (should the evidence and arguments be presented at trial), the attorneys prepare a brief, including the facts and legal arguments in support of their clients' case. The attorneys will also present submissions to the judge, based on this brief. The attorneys' role is more active, similar to litigating a case, as opposed to one that is primarily advisory in nature.

#### i) Binding Court Decisions

Various provinces and territories in Canada have instituted an option of dispute settlement aimed at alleviating the time and costs associated with holding a trial.

In the case of binding court decisions,[22] a judge meets with the concerned parties who have agreed to be bound by a decision of the court without a costly trial.

---

21 Alberta Court of Justice, "Resolution Tracks: Binding Judicial Dispute Resolution" Judicial Dispute Resolution (2022), online: www.albertacourts.ca/cj/areas-of-law/civil/claims/resolution-tracks/bjdr. In Alberta, for example, judges may give a non-binding opinion as to the decision they would render if the case were presented at trial. This may assist the parties in reaching a resolution without having to go through a trial. Binding JDRs are also available. In such cases, the parties must agree beforehand that the judge's opinion will be binding. Ontario has instituted a binding judicial dispute resolution pilot project, effective May 2021; see Ashley Saad, "Judicial Mediation in Canada: An Inspiring Success Story" Canadian Institute for the Administration of Justice (17 December 2018), online: https://ciaj-icaj.ca/en/2018/12/17/judicial-mediation-in-canada-an-inspiring-success-story.

22 Sean Fine, "Saskatchewan Judges Offer to Make Binding Decisions" *Globe and Mail* (5 October 2020), online: www.theglobeandmail.com/canada/article-judges-in-saskatchewan-offering-to-settle-legal-disputes-by-making.

The lawyers representing the parties are required to put together a brief, setting out the facts and evidence supporting them. Instead of a lengthy trial, costing thousands of dollars in legal fees and court fees, a judge, after reviewing the briefs and meeting with the parties, decides the case.

However, in instances where a judge decides that it is inappropriate to render a binding decision, as in a case where not enough evidence has been presented, the judge can decline to render a decision. Criticism has centred around strong-armed judges who speak with a great deal of authority while rights get short-circuited.

This procedure has been introduced in Saskatchewan and has been modelled on similar procedures instituted in Alberta, Newfoundland and Labrador, and Yukon.

### j) Other Means

Other methods of dispute resolution include:

#### *i) Parenting Coordination*

This is a process used to resolve ongoing conflict between separated or divorced parents, with the focus on the needs and well-being of their children. Parenting coordinators help the parties to resolve their issues. In cases where the parents are unable to reach an agreement, parenting coordinators may have decision-making powers, if they can act as an arbitrator.[23]

#### *ii) Restorative Justice*

These mechanisms involve persons charged with an offence and those who were victims of the offence. The process of restorative justice allows the parties affected by a crime to express their needs, while the offenders are encouraged to understand the extent to which they have harmed the victims and to try to repair the harm. In essence, this form of justice allows for the recovery of the affected persons and is geared to their healing. The offending parties are encouraged to accept responsibility and to repair the harm

---

23 Amanda Marsden, "What Is Parenting Coordination?" Crossroads Law (16 April 2018), online: www.crossroadslaw.ca/blog/what-is-parenting-coordination.

the victims experienced. The concerned parties, including family members and members of the community, actively participate in the process with the aim of restoration as well as prevention.[24]

#### *iii) Collaborative or Cooperative Law*

This constitutes a manner of practising law differently and changing the dynamic relationship among lawyers. Rather than focusing a law practice on litigation, the lawyers undertake collaborative efforts to settle a dispute.

In collaborative law, if the lawyers are unable to settle a case, they will cease representing their clients if the case goes to trial. In cooperative law, on the other hand, while lawyers also consent to use a collaborative approach to resolving conflict, if the case goes to trial, they will not withdraw from the case and will continue to represent their clients.[25]

## C. MEDIATION PROCESSES

### 1) Legislation Governing Private and Judicial Mediation

The process of settling disputes other than by litigation is not uniform. Legislation governing mediation varies from one jurisdiction to another, both in terms of governing private mediation processes and in terms of judicial mediations.

Private mediation processes can be voluntary or mandatory, depending on the jurisdiction in which they are practiced. Quebec, for example, foresees a voluntary and confidential dispute resolution process for the private sector. It encourages such means by requiring that parties consider private prevention and resolution processes before referring their dispute to the courts.[26] Other provinces and territories in Canada include mediation and different dispute resolution methods in their legal processes.

---

24 Department of Justice Canada, "Principles of Restorative Justice" (13 December 2021), online: www.justice.gc.ca/eng/rp-pr/cj-jp/victim/rest.html.

25 Resolution Systems Institute, "Court ADR Basics: Overview," above note 3.

26 *Code of Civil Procedure*, CQLR C-25.01, s 1(3) [*CCP*].

While the voluntary mediation system has been chosen by most jurisdictions, some compel mediation with detailed and comprehensive provisions governing the process. Ontario, for example, has adopted a position favouring mandatory mediation for most cases of civil litigation[27] and non-family actions, as well as in matters involving contested estates, trusts, and substitute decision matters,[28] before they go to trial. British Columbia has adopted mandatory mediation for certain cases, such as small claims, and requires attendance at a mediation session in other types of cases.[29]

Judicial mediation also varies from one Canadian province and territory to another with respect to the nature of the process.[30] Each province and territory has some rules that address the role of the judiciary in dispute resolution. While most provinces and territories formally recognize that the judiciary can be involved in resolving disputes, the process itself and the role that a judge plays in settlement conferences differs according to the applicable legislation.

In Quebec, for example, parties can choose a process called *conference de règlement a l'amiable* (CRA) or *settlement conference*[31] to resolve their dispute. The procedure is presided over by a judge, who helps the parties find solutions for settling their case. The process, which is held in the presence of both parties and their counsel, is interest based, non-evaluative, voluntary, informal, confidential, and free of charge.

---

27 *Courts of Justice Act*, RSO 1990; *Rules of Civil Procedure*, c C.43; *Rules of Civil Procedure*, RRO 1990, Reg 194, r 24.1

28 *Rules of Civil Procedure*, *ibid*, r 75.1.

29 In the BC Supreme Court, a Notice to Mediate process allows any party, to a range of actions, to require all other parties to the actions to mediate the matters in a dispute.

30 Saad, "Judicial Mediation in Canada," above note 21. The information regarding judicial mediation in Canada is contained in a report issued by the Canadian Institute for the Administration of Justice, following an international seminar celebrating the twentieth anniversary of judicial mediation; see Jean-François Roberge, "Emerging Trends in Access to Justice and Dispute Resolution in Canada" (2014) 4:2 *Revue d'arbitrage et de médiation/Journal of Arbitration and Mediation* at 80.

31 *CCP*, above note 26, ss. 161–65.

In Alberta, judges can take an evaluative approach or one that is highly facilitative. The process, which is voluntary, is presided over by a judge and is known as Judicial Dispute Resolution (JDR).[32]

Participants meet with a judge and discuss the background of their case and possible solutions. If no agreement is reached, the judge can provide an opinion as to the probable outcome of the case were the JDR evidence and argument to be presented at trial. The judge's opinion on any or all the issues is non-binding, unless the parties agree beforehand to hold a binding JDR, in which case the judge renders a decision at the end of the JDR.

Other provinces offer voluntary judicially assisted dispute resolution, which can include settlement conferences, neutral evaluations, and mini trials.

Although there is a lack of uniformity with respect to legislation throughout Canada, there is nevertheless recognition, by the various provincial governments, that the increased use of mediation or other forms of dispute resolution is beneficial to litigants and increases access to justice.

The process helps alleviate the problems related to the long delays that exist between the institution of an action and the trial, the high cost of litigation, and the complexity of the justice system.

It also alleviates some of the stress faced by the litigants, and ultimately results in a greater level of satisfaction on the part of the parties. This satisfaction stems from the parties being able to create solutions that not only resolve the conflict, but also meet their non-legal considerations, including the emotional aspects of their dispute.

It is not the intent in this text to provide the legislation governing dispute resolution in each province and territory. However, because of the variation that exists in legislation that governs dispute resolution methods in different jurisdictions, it is essential for lawyers to follow the provisions regarding these mechanisms that are applicable in the location in which they are practicing.

---

32 *Alberta Rules of Court*, Alta Reg 124/2010, s 4.16(1)(c) and ff.

## D. THE NATURE OF MEDIATION

### 1) Definition of Mediation

As already indicated, mediation is the means of settling a dispute with the intervention of a neutral and impartial third party, namely a mediator. The mediator's intervention can alter the dynamics of the negotiations between the parties and enable them to reach an agreement.

As explained in a previous section, mediators, in interest-based mediations, have no power to impose an agreement on disputing parties. They do not judge the case or issue any orders. They do not determine the responsibility of either party or the outcome of the case. Rather, the mediator acts as an *orchestra leader*, facilitating the discussion and helping the parties to communicate and negotiate with each other in order to reach a solution that satisfies both sides in the conflict.

In an evaluative approach, on the other hand, mediators are asked to evaluate each party's case and express their opinion on the issues in dispute, as well as what the likely outcome might be if the case went to trial.

While I will discuss the different approaches that exist in more detail in another section, the emphasis in this book, as indicated above, will be on interest-based mediation. The emphasis will also be on the process that is initiated by the parties and entirely voluntary. However, even when the mediation process is mandatory, the recommended approach for preparing for mediation and the mediation process itself remains the same.

### 2) Purpose of Mediation

The purpose of mediation for your clients is not to establish that their case is well founded. If this is your clients' objective, then it is preferable for them to go to court.

Your clients must understand that the purpose of mediation is to find a solution to their conflict that meets the interests and needs of both parties. It is not to determine who is right or who is responsible for the conflict. In fact, parties are often willing to pay money or settle by other means to avoid the time, stress, expense, delays, and inconvenience of a trial, without any admission of responsibility.

Consider, for example, a case involving a dismissal. If your client has been terminated and establishes the absence of just cause in a civil lawsuit that proceeds to trial, some amount of compensation will be ordered by the court.

However, although your client will usually seek a sum of money from the ex-employer, there may be other measures, in conjunction with a sum of money, that could satisfy your client's interests and needs.

Clients in such situations may appreciate an explanation from their ex-employers about why the employment relationship was severed. Clients may also appreciate an apology for the abruptness and the impact the decision had on them. It may be important for them to obtain a letter of recommendation. Other elements that may satisfy their needs include obtaining job retraining, outsourcing services to help them find another job, or the equipment they need to start their own business.

These means of settlement cannot be ordered by a court. Learning that such possibilities are available through mediation can be a large inducement for your clients to opt for this manner of dealing with their conflictual situation.

Even when mediation is mandatory, understanding what type of solutions can be obtained through this process can result in your clients adopting a positive attitude when they participate in the mediation.

### 3) Advantages of Mediation

Your clients should be aware of the advantages of mediation, which are numerous and include:

- the possibility of selecting an appropriate mediator;
- the rapidity of scheduling a mediation session;

- the lack of formality;
- the flexibility of the process;
- the confidential nature of the process;
- the cost being less than a trial;
- the process being less stressful than a trial;
- the process being less time consuming than a trial;
- the possibility of determining the issues to be discussed;
- the possibility of going beyond the subject matter of a lawsuit;
- the possibility of speaking directly to the other party;
- the opportunity to explain one's perspective on the case;
- the opportunity to express emotions;
- the possibility of re-establishing, maintaining, continuing, or improving an ongoing relationship;
- a better control over the process and the results than a trial;
- the avoidance of a potentially unfavourable judgment;
- the possibility of a settlement being advantageous for impacted third parties;
- the possibility of being creative and finding imaginative solutions that do not involve money;
- the possibility of finding a solution that cannot be ordered by a judge;
- the possibility of finding a satisfactory solution adapted to one's interests and needs;
- a greater satisfaction with the overall process than with a trial;
- the immediate knowledge of the outcome;
- a better compliance with the settlement; and
- most important, a solution that is *made to measure*.

## 4) Mediation Versus a Trial

There are numerous differences between a mediation and a trial. However, the essential difference between the two is their purpose. In a trial, the purpose is to determine who is right. Following the end of the hearing, the judge renders a decision.

The mediation process is aimed at re-establishing communication and ultimately satisfying the interests and needs of the parties. The purpose is to find a solution that satisfies both parties. Mediators do not render a decision or issue orders. They do not even provide an opinion unless their mandate is that of evaluative mediation.

The court process is adversarial, while mediation is collaborative. If a relationship existed prior to the conflict, it is unlikely that the relationship will be re-established after a trial. However, given that mediation is collaborative and there is an effort for the parties to work together, there is often a possibility for the parties to reconnect and continue a relationship into the future.

Trials are costly, time consuming, and stressful for the parties. There is always the risk of an unfavourable judgment for one of the parties. In the end, there is a winner and a loser. At times, both parties feel that they have lost.

Court proceedings take place in a set framework and deal only with the allegations contained in the proceedings, while mediation allows for a discussion of any aspect of a conflict. A trial ends with a judgment but it may not always resolve the conflict. Mediation, on the other hand, attempts to settle all outstanding issues between the parties.

Court proceedings are public, and judgments are published. One of the aspects of mediation that is of particular interest to many parties is the confidential nature of the process and the outcome. All discussions, as well as the offers, concessions, and admissions that are made, remain confidential and cannot be divulged by any of the participants.

Mediation costs less than a trial, takes less time, and is less stressful. Since both parties must agree on the content of an agreement, there is not a winner and a loser. We say that both parties win or that the method is a win-win process.

### 5) Mediation Versus Negotiation

Negotiation takes place regularly in litigious situations, and most lawyers are familiar with this means of dispute resolution. The discussions are aimed at convincing the other party that their client's position is well founded. Each lawyer tries to obtain the best possible results for their client at the expense of the opposing party. The lawyers generally deal with each other and report back to their clients. The clients, however, do not speak directly to each other, and the emotional aspect of the conflict is rarely taken into consideration.

This process, which is called *competitive negotiation* or *negotiation on position*, is adversarial and involves a power play between the lawyers. While mediation also involves negotiations, it is based on the parties' interests and needs. The process in mediation is collaborative. The parties, and not only the lawyers, are directly involved. The parties must work together, compromise, and look for a way of resolving their conflict. The result must not only be advantageous for one party but must also be beneficial and satisfactory for both parties.

Mediation is preferable to competitive negotiations that take place between lawyers. It allows the parties to deal with each other directly and openly. It also allows the parties to go beyond the terms of their lawsuit and deal with their relationship. Furthermore, since the parties have worked together to reach a solution, there is a greater chance that they will respect the settlement that they have reached.

There are, nevertheless, situations where competitive negotiations based on position are appropriate. Such cases include situations where there is no interest on the part of the parties to continue a relationship or where the objective of obtaining a certain item at a certain price is clear, and there are no other aspects of the conflict to take into consideration.

### 6) Mediation Versus Settlement Conferences or a JDR

Settlement conferences and judicial dispute resolution (JDR) have characteristics that are very similar to mediation. Each process has advantages and disadvantages.

The advantage of settlement conferences or JDRs is that, contrary to private mediation, where mediators charge for their services, there is no cost to the parties when they attend a settlement conference presided over by a judge. Agreements are also readily reached, given the moral authority of a judge and the impact of a judge's comments.

However, in some jurisdictions, a lawsuit must be instituted to have access to judicial mediation, whereas private mediations can take place at any stage of a conflict, even if no legal proceedings have been filed. In addition, the parties have no control over the location of the meetings presided over by a judge and less control over the scheduling, when compared to mediation. The issues are limited to what is alleged in the legal proceedings, while mediation allows the parties to deal with the root of their problems as well as broader issues that have impacted them.

In mediation, the parties can choose a mediator they believe would be best suited for their case, although the choice must be a joint one. They can choose a specialist with certain expertise, if they are of the view that this type of mediator is required. They can also choose a mediator who practices evaluative mediation, which entails giving an opinion on the case and on its outcome, if the case were to go to court.

While parties in most jurisdictions cannot choose the judge who will preside over their settlement conference, in other jurisdictions, such a choice is possible. As already indicated, in Alberta, for example, the parties together with their lawyers can select the judge who will preside over a JDR. They can also request that the judge provide an opinion on the case.

Either mediation or a settlement conference is a valid option, depending on the circumstances involved in each case, such as the cost, the available dates offered, whether a specialist is sought, and so on.

### 7) Mediation Versus Other Methods

Other dispute resolution methods have been outlined above. Arbitration, while less costly and more flexible than a trial, remains an adversarial process with a decision rendered at the end of the process. Consequently, it is akin to a trial when compared with the mediation process, although it is more flexible and offers the possibility of choosing a specialist in the field of the conflict.

The combination of mediation and arbitration offers the advantages of mediation, but both med/arb and arb/med involve some aspect of an adversarial process, which runs contrary to the concept of a collaborative means of resolving conflict.

While both early neutral evaluation and the mini trial provide an assessment of the parties' strengths and weaknesses, a conjecture as to the probable outcome of the conflict if it were to go to trial, and a possible solution, neither method involves a collaborative approach, which is beneficial to a mutually satisfactory settlement.

## 8) Your Clients' Choice

Clients will usually be stressed and emotional when they consult a lawyer, whether they wish to institute a lawsuit or they have been sued. Most often, they are not aware that there are alternative means of dealing with their conflict, other than resorting to the courts. Therefore, it is important to determine whether a trial or a means of dispute resolution is the option to propose. Proposing dispute resolution, rather than a trial, depends on what your client is seeking.

If your clients' aim is to establish their rights, create a precedent, seek publicity, or immediately protect their property, then the judicial system is the appropriate choice. If they want to obtain a decision with a process that is more flexible than the courts, the appropriate choice is arbitration. In other cases, different dispute resolution processes are more advantageous, and the various options should be presented.

Ultimately, your clients should make the choice once you have provided them with an explanation of the existing methods for dealing with conflict. Armed with sufficient information, they will be able to make an informed decision.

### 9) The Lawyer's Role in Mediation

It is not only important for your clients to understand that there are other means of dealing with their legal issues than going to court, but it is also equally important for your clients to understand that your role in dispute resolution differs from that of a litigator.

As litigators in an adversarial system, lawyers tend to be combative and aggressive, making every effort to successfully present their clients' position before a court and win the case. However, as a lawyer involved in mediation or settlement conferences, you must act in a collaborative manner to find a solution that will be satisfactory to your clients as well as to the other party.

It is useful to know that it is the parties who take centre stage. They are the ones who will relate the facts of the case and express their perspectives as to what transpired leading to the dispute. They are also the ones who, with your help and the help of the other lawyer, will negotiate with each other, will be proposing options for a settlement, and will ultimately decide upon the content of their agreement.

As counsel, you will not be presenting the legal aspects of the case (unless the mediator has been hired to provide an evaluation) and you will not be questioning your clients or cross-examining the other party. Mediation is not the appropriate forum for this way of proceeding.

Although it appears that you will be taking a back seat during the mediation, you retain your role as counsel. Your mandate also involves assisting both your clients and the mediator in finding a reasonable solution.

You play an essential part in the mediation process by guiding your clients and helping them find a solution to their conflict, from the outset to its conclusion, by doing the following:

- explaining the nature of the process and its advantages so that clients will understand how the mediation session will take place and what solutions are possible;
- identifying your clients' goals;
- initiating the mediation process, including choosing a mediator with the opposing party;

- reviewing the mediation contract to determine whether all aspects have been included;
- preparing for the mediation session—for example, deciding who will participate, determining the interests and needs of the parties, discussing strategy, and so on;
- preparing an opening statement, if required;
- preparing your clients to relate their version of the facts, to express their emotions, and to participate in the mediation session effectively;
- preparing your clients to formulate and respond to criticism;
- helping your clients present proposals with creativity;
- determining when it is appropriate or necessary to ask for a break or a caucus during the mediation;
- intervening in helping your clients save face or defusing their anger;
- helping your clients negotiate options;
- helping your clients evaluate the proposals put forward;
- requesting caucuses, when needed;
- assisting when an impasse occurs;
- helping your clients select appropriate options for settlement;
- ensuring that your clients have a realistic vision of a potential solution;
- presenting your clients with a comparison of the advantages and the costs involved if the parties do not settle;
- explaining the fiscal impact of a settlement;
- providing advice throughout the mediation;
- protecting your clients' interests and rights;
- helping your clients obtain a satisfactory outcome;
- preparing the agreement or participating with the opposing attorney in drafting an agreement, if a settlement of the conflict is reached; and
- taking steps to enforce the agreement, if appropriate.

The initial steps, as well as the preparation for a mediation, are essential for the success of a mediation.

*chapter two*

# Initiating the Mediation Process

When I was first approached by lawyers to determine whether I would accept a mediation mandate, I indicated my availability and my rate. I soon realized that the lawyers, who were not sufficiently familiar with the process, needed to know more. I began to make suggestions and provide information that would facilitate the process.

Amongst others, I suggested that each lawyer advise their opponent that their client was open to the idea of settling the case. If the opposing lawyer was of the same view, I recommended that the lawyer list a couple of potential mediators to be contacted. If the lawyer only suggested me to preside over the mediation session, the other party might be concerned that I would favour the party who had selected me.

I added information about my background, certification, experience, and approach, as well as whether the mediation will take place in person or virtually. If the session takes place in person, the lawyer should be aware not only of the location but also of other aspects regarding the facilities as well. These details are essential for a lawyer to know before providing a mandate to a mediator. Unfortunately, many lawyers fail to ask the appropriate questions.

This chapter concerns all the information that lawyers need in order to raise the subject of mediation with their clients, take the necessary steps to initiate the process with an opponent, choose an acceptable mediator, determine the appropriateness of the location, handle virtual mediation sessions, ask about the duration and number of sessions, and so on.

❋ ❋ ❋ ❋ ❋

The following are the tasks that should be performed to initiate the process:

- Propose mediation to your clients as a means of dealing with their conflict by informing them as to the nature of mediation and, in jurisdictions where mediation is voluntary, of the advantages of such a procedure.
- Propose mediation (where the process is voluntary) to the opposite party or to their lawyer.
- Prepare a list of mediators and consider a few who are most appropriate. Select one together with opposing counsel.
- Determine the location of the mediation session together with opposing counsel, in cases where the mediation is not held virtually.
- Ensure that you have the necessary means to conduct a virtual hearing, if that is the method determined for the mediation.
- Determine the scheduling of the mediation session.
- Review the mediation contract.
- Review the confidentiality agreement.

Each of these tasks is considered in greater detail below.

## A. PROPOSING MEDIATION TO YOUR CLIENTS

### 1) Explain Mediation and Its Benefits to Your Clients

In the past, when clients consulted a litigation lawyer to institute an action or to be defended from an action taken against them, the approach for the lawyer to take was clear. It involved drafting proceedings, carrying out examinations, and eventually representing their clients in court.

As indicated in the introduction, the role of litigation lawyers has evolved over time. With a change in culture, it is appropriate to adopt a different approach, based on the concept of *participative justice.*[1] This concept favours a new vision of justice, which provides greater consideration to the persons involved and attempts to respond to their interests and needs.

You can begin by explaining the applicable law to your clients, as well as the strengths and weaknesses of their case, and the various aspects of litigating the conflict. However, rather than end your discussion with an explanation as to how you will begin the litigation process or how you will defend your clients, you should explain the existence of mediation as well as the other forms of dispute resolution.

In locations where mediation is voluntary, you should indicate the importance given to mediation in the legal system and the fact that it is encouraged as a means of dealing with conflict. Other information to be given to your clients includes an explanation of what mediation entails, the benefits of this process, and the satisfaction experienced by the participants.

In jurisdictions where mediation is mandatory, it is essential to explain to your clients the obligation to participate in the process, how it will transpire, the costs involved, and what will occur if the case does not settle.

Therefore, it is appropriate to begin by explaining the nature of mediation and the numerous advantages to resolving their conflict by this means.

### AN EXAMPLE OF A MEDIATION PROPOSAL

The following is an example of a mediation proposal you can present to your clients in jurisdictions where mediation is voluntary, with the appropriate modifications when mediation is mandatory:

I want to discuss the possibility of settling your case by means of mediation and proposing this means to the other party.

---

1 Miville Tremblay, "La Justice Participative" (2023–24) *Collection des Habiletés, Justice Participative*, Barreau du Québec at 8–9.

Mediation involves having a third person, a certified mediator, who is neutral and impartial, help you and the opposite party communicate with each other, present proposals for settlement, negotiate, and find a solution that is satisfactory for both of you.

This is not a sign of weakness on your part. The process is voluntary; both parties must agree to participate in the session. However, it is important for you to know that our legal system encourages mediation as a means of settling disputes.

In the case of mandatory mediation: The law requires you to attend a mediation session, which is conducted by a mediator in the private sector. Specific time periods are set for selecting a mediator and for the mediation to take place. If you fail to attend, you may be subject to sanctions imposed by the court.

During the mediation process, whether it is voluntary or mandatory, you will be explaining your version of the facts to the other party and negotiating with them. You will have the opportunity to speak directly to the other party and express your feelings about what occurred. I will ensure that you are prepared so that you will be able to participate effectively in the mediation.

My role will be different than what my role would be before the courts. I will be present to help you find a solution to your case that you are comfortable with.

I will try to collaborate, rather than be combative. This does not mean that I will not represent you. I will provide advice and make sure that your rights are respected. If you reach a settlement, I will participate in the drafting of the agreement.

There are many advantages to mediation:

- You will have the possibility of selecting an appropriate mediator.
- You will get a date for the mediation session relatively quickly, and you will be involved in selecting the date.
- The process is less formal and more flexible than a trial.
- The process will provide you with the opportunity to express your feelings or emotions about what occurred in your case.
- The process will be less costly than a trial.
- The process will be less stressful than a trial.

- Mediation will be less time consuming than a trial.
- The mediation process is confidential; your name and the facts of your dispute will not be made public.
- You will have the possibility of determining the issues to be discussed as well as the possibility of resolving issues that go beyond the subject matter of your lawsuit.
- You will have the opportunity to speak directly to the opposite party.
- You will also have the opportunity to explain your perspective on the conflict.
- Mediation provides the possibility of re-establishing, maintaining, continuing, or improving your relationship with the other party.
- You will have input in the process, giving you better control over the process than in a trial.
- You will have the opportunity to be creative and find imaginative solutions.
- You will avoid a potentially unfavourable judgment.
- If third parties are involved in your case, a settlement can be advantageous for them.
- If you settle, you will know the outcome immediately and you will not have to wait for a judgment, which could take several months.
- There is more likelihood of compliance with a settlement than a judgment.
- If you settle and the other party violates the agreement, you can present a motion (or an application, depending on the circumstances) to the court to have the agreement enforced. (In Quebec, you can ask that a judge homologate the agreement, that is, take cognizance of your agreement, which will give it the same force as a judgment of the court.)

And the most important aspect of mediation is that you will have control over the outcome of the mediation. You will be able to determine the solution that meets your interests and needs and works for both you and the opposite party. This may even involve a solution that cannot be ordered by a judge, such as an apology, the provision of services or products, or other innovative proposals, rather than a sum of money. It may also be possible to reconnect with the other party or re-draft a contractual relationship that falls outside the scope of your immediate problem or your litigation.

Do you have any questions?

Are you willing to consider the possibility of mediation?

If so, we will propose mediation to the other party, and if they agree, then we will discuss how we will proceed, including the choice of a mediator, our preparation, our strategy, and so on.

In the case of a mandatory mediation: I will prepare a short list of mediators whom I consider appropriate for your case, and I will contact the lawyer representing the opposite party and ask the lawyer to choose one of these mediators. The mediation session will be held within a short period of time after that. Then we will prepare for the mediation. I will explain how it will proceed. I will ensure that you are ready to present the facts of the case and negotiate with the other party. I will also be present and advise you throughout the process.

### 2) Explaining Judicial Mediation

In locations where judicial mediation exists, it is appropriate to explain to your clients that it is possible to opt for another type of dispute mechanism, namely judicial mediation, which is known as a settlement conference or judicial dispute resolution.

You should explain the advantages of choosing judicial mediation, including the fact there is no charge for the services of the judge and because of a judge's authority, a high rate of settlement normally takes place. While the disadvantages are not numerous, you should mention that, with few exceptions, your clients cannot choose the location or the judge who will preside over the mediation. There may also be less flexibility in scheduling and the issues generally cannot go beyond what is alleged in the legal proceedings.

As already indicated in Chapter 1, mediation sessions with a private mediator and those presided over by a judge are remarkably similar in nature. Either option can be instrumental in bringing about a settlement.

### 3) The Desire to Settle

It may seem evident that parties who attend a mediation session want to settle. When both parties are intent in resolving their conflict, they are most often successful in finding a solution. However, the simple fact that both parties are involved in the process does not necessarily mean that they will settle. Mediation does not invariably result in an agreement.

Whether the situation is one where a conflict has already taken place or simply one where the parties are trying to reach an agreement concerning the terms of a contract, future relations, visiting rights, or a course of action, there must be the will to find common ground.

Consider the following example:

> A well-known artist has a painting to sell, and a potential customer, having seen the painting, asks how much it will cost. The artist indicates that the price is $20,000. The potential customer makes an offer of $10,000, which is considerably less than the asking price. The artist then makes a counter proposal of $18,000, which in the mind of the potential customer is still rather high. The potential customer considers the possible options. The potential customer decides the artwork is not essential and consequently, does not offer more. The artist, who does not want the value of his artwork to decrease, refuses the offer and maintains his original counteroffer of $18,000. Since both parties have maintained their last offers, there is a stalemate, and no deal is reached.

In this example, what is clear is that neither party has a real incentive to change their position and reach an agreement. The artist does not want to devalue the artwork and is therefore not motivated to sell at any price, while for the potential customer, the artwork is overly expensive. The potential customer has enough artwork and is not interested in paying any more than the original offer. In short, there was no real desire for either party to find common ground. Put differently, there was a lack of sufficient interest and need to motivate either party to come to an agreement.

Let us consider another scenario involving the artwork:

> If the potential customer genuinely wants the artwork, the customer will try to bring down the price but, ultimately, will offer an amount that approaches what the artist is seeking, in order to conclude the deal. At the same time, the potential customer may seek some modalities regarding the payment, as, for example, requesting that the payment be made in instalments. Alternatively, if the artist needs money, the artist will be more willing to compromise and sell the painting at a price closer to what the potential customer is prepared to pay. At the same time, the artist may demand a confidentiality agreement regarding the price, in order not to devalue the artwork.

If your clients state that they are willing to participate in a mediation, they must understand that there are compromises to be made and that the goal is to find a means of putting the conflict or the lawsuit to rest. Even where mediation is mandatory, given its benefits, it is most often in your clients' interest to try to find a means of reaching an agreement with the other party.

### 4) Areas in Which Mediation Is Practiced

Traditionally, in Canada, mediation has been associated with the field of labour relations involving management and unions as well as with family law conflicts. The practice of mediation may have developed in these areas because of the early adoption of legislation dealing with the resolution of conflicts.[2] The practice of mediation in these fields may also have developed because of

2 *The Conciliation Act*, SC 1900, c 24, which created the Canada Department of Labour with a mandate to assist unions and employers in the prevention and resolution of disputes, was adopted in 1900; in the area of family law, the *Divorce Act*, RSC 1985, c 3 (2nd Supp), was adopted in 1986 and included a provision obliging every legal adviser to encourage their client to attempt to resolve their conflict through a family dispute resolution process.

the parties' ongoing relationship[3] and the need for them to have mechanisms to resolve their disputes.

Mediation is an important means of dealing with conflict in ongoing relationships or relations that may continue in the future. This would encompass disputes between companies that do business with each other and are dependent on each other in terms of services or products. It may involve associates or business partners within a corporation. It is also useful in relationships involving landlord and tenants, in franchising arrangements, and in large construction projects.

More recently, mediation is used in virtually every imaginable field of endeavour. It is regularly sought in commercial conflicts as well as in civil disputes, whether they involve consumer affairs, service contracts, insurance claims, or any other area. It can involve not only lawyers but also specialists in areas other than law, such as medicine, accounting, engineering, architecture, agriculture, education, human resources, finance, and many others.

Mediation has been made available to parties not only by the courts but by quasi-judicial tribunals as well. The awareness of dispute resolution has increased considerably over the years and is widely accepted.

## 5) Cases Where Mediation Is Not Recommended

Most cases allow for mediation or a settlement conference. There are cases where mediation is not always recommended. Such cases include the following:

- Your clients seek a legal precedent.
- A principle is involved for your clients.
- Your clients seek publicity for their case.
- The publicity that would be involved in a judgment would be in your clients' favour.

3 While couples may not want anything to do with each other, when children are involved, there is a need for the parents to continue to deal with each other in the interest of their children.

- The intervention of the court is needed to rapidly protect property.
- A case of fraud is involved, or the other party is in bad faith.
- The claim involves a small sum of money, and the cost of mediation is disproportionate to the amount of the claim.
- Your clients do not want to be in the same room as the other party.
- Your clients are too vulnerable and easily influenced.
- Your clients are victims of violence or threats by their partners or spouses.
- Your clients' expectations are unreasonable or unrealistic.
- The claim of the opposing party is clearly prescribed.
- The case involves a public authority, and the issue falls under a provision that is of public order and cannot be negotiated.
- A transaction or a settlement has already been concluded by the parties.
- Your clients are convinced they have a good case and are not sufficiently motivated to settle.

While there appears to be many cases where lawyers are reluctant to recommend mediation, several of these situations could be removed from the above list if lawyers, who are knowledgeable about mediation, properly counsel and assist their clients. For example, there is no guarantee that clients will win a case or that a judgment will be in your clients' favour. Vulnerable clients can participate in mediations if they are protected by competent counsel. Having a claim involving a small sum of money is not an impediment to mediation, as evidenced by Small Claims Court mediations. Those clients who do not want to be in the same room as the opposing party can nevertheless participate in a mediation session if it is carried out in caucuses.

In summary, mediation is beneficial to opposing parties in most instances. There are very few cases where mediation should not be recommended.

### 6) Advantages of Mediation for Lawyers

Lawyers in jurisdictions where mediation is optional are often unfamiliar with the mediation process and their role in representing their clients in such situations. As a result, they are reluctant to recommend mediation to their clients. In addition, the revenue from mediation is a great deal less than that obtained from a trial, particularly when a lengthy trial is foreseen. Because of this, many lawyers do not raise mediation as an option, and since most clients are not aware of this possibility, they do not request it either.

However, despite this, representing clients in mediations in fact has certain benefits for lawyers. First of all, lawyers have found that what they lose in revenue from each case is compensated by the volume of cases that they can handle in mediations. Further, if they fail to pursue mediations and gain experience in this area, other professionals will occupy the domain. As a result, they will lose clients.

Accordingly, there is every reason for lawyers to familiarize themselves with the process and to encourage their clients to participate in mediation.

## B. PROPOSING MEDIATION TO THE OPPONENT

In those jurisdictions where mediation is voluntary, even after your client has accepted the idea, the other party must also agree to participate before the mediation can take place.

As indicated in Chapter 1, proposing mediation to the opposite party is no longer considered to be an indication of a weak case or a weakness on your part, as a lawyer. Mediation and other options are well-known and encouraged by our courts across Canada. Therefore, contrary to the situation that prevailed years ago, you should not have to convince the opposing counsel that your proposal to mediate a conflict has nothing to do with the merits of your clients' case or your ability to represent them.

### 1) When to Propose Mediation

When is the appropriate time is to propose mediation to the opposite party? The possibilities range from the outset of the conflict to any time after the proceedings have been instituted but before the trial. The following examines the pros and cons of two different time frames.

#### a) Immediately, Before Proceedings Are Instituted

Many lawyers and mediators consider that it is preferable for mediation to take place as soon as possible once a dispute arises. Given the changed legal culture in which mediation or settlement conferences are becoming more and more the norm, the opposite party, if already represented by a lawyer, will not be surprised by a proposal to mediate.

Parties may be open to settlement discussions at the outset of a dispute, before instituting legal proceedings, for many reasons, including the fact that they are more flexible at an early stage of a conflict. With time, the conflict often degenerates and becomes more difficult to resolve.

The parties may wish to resolve their issues before their legal costs mount, or they may be inclined to consider mediation early on once they learn of the lengthy delays that are involved before their case is scheduled for trial. In addition, the element of stress may play a role. The parties may be anxious to resolve their issue, rather than have it hanging over them for a considerable amount of time.

If the choice is made to broach the subject of mediation before instituting proceedings, one way of handling the proposal is to send an informal letter to the other party, stating your clients' position, but suggesting that the parties settle their dispute amicably by means of mediation.

A more typical way of dealing with the matter is to include the possibility of settling the conflict in your demand letter. After outlining the salient facts of your clients' case and indicating that, on behalf of your clients, you are holding the opposing party responsible for your clients' damages, you can add that your clients are open to a dispute resolution mechanism for settling the conflict.

### AN EXAMPLE OF A DEMAND LETTER CONTAINING A PROPOSAL FOR MEDIATION

Consequently, failing to pay $ xxx on or before (the date), the necessary legal proceedings will be instituted against you, without further notice or delay.

Under reserve of our claim against you, and in order to resolve this dispute quickly and in an amicable manner, we are authorized to advise you that our clients are open to settlement discussions before instituting legal proceedings. Accordingly, if such an approach is acceptable to you and you agree to participate in mediation, please advise the undersigned on or before (the date) and we will contact you to begin the process of selecting a mediator, a location if the mediation session is held in person, and a date for the mediation.

In the case of a traditional demand letter, the recipient typically consults a lawyer, who also has the possibility of raising mediation as an option, even if there is no mention of such a process in the demand letter. Therefore, if you represent clients who are threatened with a lawsuit, you can deny the claim, but add that your clients are open to participate in a mediation and suggest this as an approach to the opposing party.

### AN EXAMPLE OF A MEDIATION PROPOSAL PRESENTED IN RESPONSE TO A TRADITIONAL DEMAND LETTER

Consequently, as indicated above, our clients deny all responsibility with respect to your allegations and will vigorously contest any legal proceedings that are instituted.

However, under reserve of our denial of responsibility and our intended vigorous contestation, I wish to advise you that our clients have authorized us to explore with you the possibility of participating in a mediation session, with the aim of settling this dispute rapidly. If you are interested in this approach, as a means of reaching an amiable solution, you can contact the undersigned on or before (the date) to discuss the manner of proceeding, including the selection of a mediator, the timing, and the location of the mediation session, if held in person.

If the parties choose to participate in mediation prior to the institution of a lawsuit, they may agree to waive prescription and the benefit of the time elapsed for prescription purposes.

### b) Later, After Proceedings Have Been Instituted

Where mediation is voluntary, there are instances where it is preferable to choose mediation after the institution of a lawsuit. In some instances, particularly those cases that are complex, you, as counsel, may wish to obtain more information from the other party to better understand their position and be prepared to respond to it. In this scenario, you may wish to wait until both parties have filed their proceedings and examinations or discoveries have taken place.

As well, several factors may impact your clients' decision to choose mediation after the litigation process has begun, even if they were not interested at the outset.

These factors include a situation where the parties were initially not prepared to face each other, but the hostility has decreased over time. Your clients may become concerned with the rising costs of the litigation and with ongoing stress. They may also be concerned with the time involved in the process and the impact of a lengthy trial on their business, profession, or job.

Another possibility is that the issue which was paramount to your clients when they first consulted you may have abated, with changed circumstances in their life, such that the issue no longer has the same importance for them.

Consider, for example, a case where a couple purchases a home and suffers a leak in their roof shortly after taking possession of the property. As a result, they sue the vendor. However, several years later, before the case goes to trial, the purchasers buy another home and move. They may be less motivated to pursue their lawsuit than they were when they first discovered the problem and consequently be willing to participate in a mediation session.

The fact that your clients do not choose to go to mediation when the conflict first arises does not preclude them from choosing mediation or a settlement conference at a later point during the litigation process.

On the other hand, it should be noted that the passage of time may have a negative impact on the parties. The parties can become more rigid and convinced of their respective positions. Once they have spent a considerable amount of time and money preparing for trial, they may simply choose to submit their case to a judge.

As well, in instances where multiple proceedings are involved, the parties often develop greater and greater animosity toward each other, such that they no longer are interested in settling their case.

Even when your clients have indicated that they want their *day in court*, this does not prevent you from raising the subject of mediation again before trial or discussing the possibility of a settlement conference led by a judge. Reiterating the advantages of these means of settlement can potentially induce your clients to reconsider their options.

## C. CHOICE OF A MEDIATOR

In private mediation, the parties are free to choose their mediator. The decision must be a joint one. When you choose a mediator, you must decide whether you are seeking an individual whose approach corresponds to that of classic mediation or facilitation, evaluation, or transformative mediation.

In addition, you may consider whether you are seeking an individual who is a specialist with expertise in a particular field or whether you wish to hire a mediator who is a generalist with a background in law.

Other attributes include the potential mediator's training, certification, style, experience, availability, fees, reputation, and whether there exists a conflict of interest, any one of which may be an important consideration for your client.

When judicial mediation is involved, you may or may not have the choice of the judge who will preside over the mediation or settlement conference, depending on the jurisdiction where you are located. Moreover, whether the judge's approach is interest-based or evaluative will also depend on the location in which the judicial mediation takes place.

These attributes should be considered when choosing a mediator.

### 1) Training and Certification of the Mediator

It is prudent to select a mediator who has obtained the requisite training and has been certified by a recognized professional association. Mediators can receive their training at certain universities[4] and colleges, provincial bar associations, and ADR organizations or institutions.[5]

Similarly, certification and/or listing in a roster of mediators[6] can be obtained from Canadian provincial bar associations and various institutions after the necessary courses and other requirements have been successfully completed. Various organizations in the United States provide training and certification to become

4 Programs exist at various Canadian universities, such as McGill University, University of Sherbrooke, and York University, to name only a few. In the United States, Harvard University, Pepperdine University, Northwestern University, and many others offer dispute resolution programs.

5 Programs are offered by various organizations, including the ADR Institute of Canada, the Canadian Institute for Conflict Resolution, Institut de Médiation et Arbitrage de Québec, and the Justice Institute of British Columbia, as well as other institutions across the country. Numerous organizations in the United States and in Europe offer courses and training to become mediators.

6 The availability of rosters varies from one Canadian province to another. For example, in Ontario a roster can be obtained from the Superior Court of Justice, the Office of the Local Mediation Coordinator, or the Ministry of the Attorney General. In Quebec, the bar and the Institut d'arbitrage et médiation provide lists of certified mediators.

professional mediators, such as the National Association of Certified Mediators and the American Association of Mediators.

While most certified mediators are lawyers, others come from a variety of backgrounds and include social workers, psychologists, bankers, businesspeople, health care specialists, IT specialists, and many other professionals. Mediators in fields other than law, such as social workers and psychologists, are frequently called upon to mediate in family conflicts.

Irrespective of whether you are seeking a generalist or a specialist, you should verify whether the mediator you have selected has been appropriately trained. You should also ensure that the mediator is recognized by a pertinent or established organization.

### a) Approach of the Mediator

There are several models that mediators can use to approach a case.[7] They vary with respect to the role of the mediator, the parties, and their lawyers, and with respect to the objectives that are sought.

The models include classical or facilitative mediation, evaluative mediation, and transformative mediation. Since parties usually seek the approach of classical mediation or, alternatively, an evaluation of their conflict, only the classical and evaluative approaches are described below.

#### *i) Classic Approach*

This approach is based on collaborative negotiation. It is oriented toward the parties' interests and needs, and a mutually satisfactory solution for both. The parties' interests are interdependent. There is an attempt to maintain an equilibrium with respect to the power between the parties and their influence.

---

7 Helene de Kovachich, "La Médiation Privée et la Conciliation Judiciare" (2023–24) *Collection des Habilités, Justice Participative*, Barreau du Québec 79 at 83–84; Zena Zumeta, "Styles of Mediation: Facilitative, Evaluative, and Transformative Mediation" *DCBA Brief* (27 February 2018), online: www.aboutrsi.org/library/styles-of-mediation-facilitative-evaluative-and-transformative-mediation.

Mediators use a structured process. They listen actively and generally use the plenary sessions, where both parties are present, as well as caucuses, where the mediators meet separately with each party. They pose questions to obtain each party's version of the conflict, search for the underlying interests of the parties, and favour dialogue to explore various options for settlement. They do not give their own advice or opinion as to the outcome of the case; rather, they help the parties develop their own propositions to resolve their conflict and evaluate the proposals put forward. Their intervention favours a solution that is satisfactory to both parties.

It should be noted that some mediators refer to this approach as pure mediation or facilitation. The majority, however, call this method classic mediation.

Supporters consider that this approach empowers the parties and helps them to resolve their conflict, while critics contend that this method takes too long and may end without an agreement.

#### *ii) Evaluative Mediation*

This type of mediation is oriented toward a judicial solution. The process involves the management of the dispute and a neutral evaluation of the case. At the outset, mediators use the same techniques as in a classical mediation, but following this, they consider the possible outcome of the conflict.

The mediators are concerned with the legal rights of the parties rather than their interests and needs. The mediators evaluate the strengths and weaknesses of the parties' respective positions. Then, based on their professional knowledge of the field in litigation, and their prediction of what a judge would likely decide, mediators give their opinion with respect to the probable outcome of the case. They then propose a solution that is not binding on the parties. However, they encourage the parties to settle based on their proposed solution or on a similar one.

Proponents of this type of mediation claim that clients want a resolution of their case if they cannot settle on their own. Critics, however, are concerned that evaluative mediators may provide an inaccurate opinion on a case. They also maintain that evaluative mediators tend to be coercive and put an excessive amount of pressure on the parties to reach an agreement. In reality, most mediators practice a little of both the classical method and the evaluative method, depending on their skills and what would be the most effective approach for the parties.

### b) Style of the Mediator

Mediators' styles vary. Some are extremely outgoing and have a strong presence throughout the process, while others are quieter and more effacing.

Some mediators prefer a cooperative approach and spend almost the totality of the mediation time in plenary sessions, working with both parties together. Other mediators will place the parties in separate rooms and shuttle back and forth between them, transmitting the positions and offers from one party to the other. This latter method, where mediators meet separately with each party and their lawyer (or, with the consent of the parties, separately with just the lawyers) is known as a caucus.

Although mediators should not provide their opinion on a case, unless they have been hired to provide a neutral evaluation, some mediators focus on the legal aspects of the dispute, while the majority tends to focus on meeting the interests and needs of each party. For most, neutrality is one of the most important characteristics of their role. However, according to rumours, some mediators have a tendency to influence the parties so that they adopt a particular solution.

Other differences in style include the way mediators handle the session. They may encourage both the lawyers and the parties to actively take part in the process, or they may relegate the lawyers to the background.

It is important for you to select a mediator whose approach and style corresponds the best with your clients' personalities and their needs. It is also essential that the mediator, who is given a mandate, is accepted by your clients and has their full confidence.

### c) Attributes of the Mediator

Mediators have different personalities. Irrespective of this characteristic, most parties want someone who is a good listener, who comprehends quickly and easily, who is readily able to summarize the facts presented by both parties, and who appears empathetic. There is always an interest in a mediator who makes the parties feel at ease and has good psychological skills in dealing with people.

For many, it is preferable to engage a mediator who is optimistic, energetic, and determined. The capacity to deal with various types of behaviour, ranging from the party who is tearful or reluctant to talk to the party who is forceful and aggressive, is also seen as an important attribute. Others are more comfortable dealing with someone who has persuasive skills or an engaging personality and charm.

While there are different attributes that parties might like a mediator to have, the essential ones are the capacity to interact well with the parties, the ability to gain their confidence, and the skill of being able to assist the parties in reaching an agreement.

### d) Expertise of the Mediator

The expertise of the mediator in a particular discipline may or may not be an important issue. In many cases, which could potentially result in litigation or instances where litigation has already begun, having a mediator with a legal background preside over the mediation is adequate, particularly when the issues are readily comprehensible. Included in this category are the myriad civil and commercial law cases that are regularly filed in court.

Other cases will benefit from a mediator's expertise in a conflict. Specialists are particularly relevant in cases where the expertise of the mediator is key to understanding the subject matter. For example, in cases dealing with labour relations, as opposed to employment law, parties will be more comfortable with a mediator who is familiar with collective bargaining issues as well as the vocabulary used (for example, issues and terms like *the scope of the bargaining unit*, *a closed shop*, or the breach of *a union security clause*), as opposed to an individual who has no knowledge of these notions or the meaning of various terms.

The same would apply to technical issues and the complexities involved in a case. Consider, for example, a dispute regarding an aviation design or a structural problem in a high-rise building that is being built, where an engineer would be an appropriate choice and would comprehend terms such as *lateral loads* and *cantilever motions of a building*. Similarly, depending on the nature of the conflict, the parties may want a mediator with expertise in areas such as finance, complex international commercial transactions, or disputes involving intellectual property, to name a few.

Having a specialist preside over the mediation does not guarantee that a settlement will be reached. However, in cases where special knowledge is concerned, the parties will have more confidence in a mediator who is familiar with the issues and who does not require lengthy explanations in order to assist the parties.

Accordingly, you must decide whether an expert is needed for your clients' dispute. If that is the case, there are many different specialties from which to choose.

Examples are numerous and wide ranging and include specialists in every conceivable field, including newer issues involving the environment, Indigenous peoples, and IT problems. It is therefore possible to select a professional with the requisite expertise who will meet the requirements and needs related to your clients' situation.

#### e) Availability of the Mediator

Many mediators are available to provide their services within a short period of time. There are others, particularly those who are well-known, who are not available to preside over mediation sessions for many months to come.

The question then arises as to how important it is for your clients to have the conflict resolved quickly. Various considerations will enter your decision. Some situations are time critical such as a construction issue, which must be resolved before the remainder of the building is completed, or the question of which school a child will attend when divorcing parents plan to live in different cities.

Other considerations involve the possibility of the problem becoming more aggravated as time goes on, the financial aspects becoming more onerous for your clients with long delays, your clients' ability to handle the stress of the conflict over a longer period, and so on. Once you have selected the type of mediator you would like to have, you should consider their availability and your clients' needs.

### f) Cost of the Mediator

The rates charged by mediators vary from one person to another, in the same way that lawyers charge different rates depending on their years of experience, expertise, and reputation. Another factor is related to the location of the mediation. The cost of a mediator in a large urban centre, in all probability, will be higher than in a small town. In those jurisdictions where mediation is mandatory, the cost is often set for a mediator who is on the roster of the program established by the jurisdiction in question.

Since the parties generally share the cost of a mediation, and since your clients must assume their share, you should be aware of the hourly rate or the daily rate charged by the mediator as well as any additional fees or expenses that may be charged, before offering the mediator a mandate. This will allow your clients to make an informed decision regarding your suggestion of a mediator and not face an invoice that is higher than expected at the end of the process.

### g) Reputation of the Mediator

Certain mediators are better known than others. Mediators generally do not have the same authority as adjudicators or judges. However, parties will generally feel comfortable with a mediator who is experienced and is well-known.

In order to develop the necessary trust, the parties must perceive the mediator as a person who has the skills to help them resolve their dispute, listens well, is empathetic, shows an understanding of the issues involved, is respectful and impartial, and genuinely appears to care about each party's feelings and concerns.

Highly reputable mediators are known for their ability to quickly grasp the essence of the problem at stake, and they are able to successfully bring about settlements, even in complex cases. They know how to demonstrate that they have heard and understood each party's perspective and concerns, while at the same time retaining their impartiality.

With these capabilities, mediators can rapidly gain the confidence of the parties, who will then be more willing to openly express their emotions, confide in the mediator, and divulge their interests and needs.

It is not unusual to try to engage the services of a well-known mediator. However, such mediators are necessarily sought after, particularly since parties tend to trust them from the outset. Consequently, these mediators may not be available for considerable periods of time, and their fees may be extremely high.

Your choice will necessarily depend on your willingness to wait for the availability of a well-known mediator and your clients' capacity and willingness to pay the higher fees.

#### h) Absence of a Conflict of Interest

Mediators must be neutral and impartial. To assume their role and inspire confidence, there cannot be any conflict of interest between your clients and the mediator or between you and the mediator.

While mediators in the classical format do not provide their opinion on the outcome of the dispute, they nevertheless must not have a personal, financial, or business relationship with either party. If one of the parties has a relationship with the mediator, the other party will necessarily feel at a disadvantage and may assume that the mediator will favour the party with whom they have ties.

It is also important for mediators not to have any interest in the conflict itself or its outcome to avoid any concern about their independence. It is not sufficient that there is no actual conflict of interest. Perception matters. If either party perceives there to be a conflict of interest, that fact alone should be the basis for not selecting that particular mediator for your case.

In summary, the neutrality of mediators is of utmost importance. Any concern about the impartiality of a mediator will necessarily undermine the process. Accordingly, if mediators are aware of any issue that could potentially cause a problem for the parties, they should raise it, and if either party or lawyer considers that this issue constitutes a problem, they should ask that the mediator withdraw from the case.

#### i) The Selection

Your choice of a mediator should take into consideration the various aspects listed above. In considering a mediator for a given case, select a trained and certified mediator who meets your clients' needs in terms of style and expertise, who has an approach that is appropriate to the result you are seeking, who is available, who charges fees that are acceptable, and who does not present a conflict of interest with you or your clients.

Different cases will call for mediators with differing expertise and approaches. Try to determine whether the selected mediator is the right one for your clients and for the issue involved. In your search for an appropriate mediator, speak to colleagues about their experiences with various mediators. You should also consider contacting the mediator you are considering hiring and asking for information that will provide you with the knowledge you need to make an informed decision.

### D. LOCATION AND SETTING FOR THE MEDIATION

A mediation can be held virtually or in person. In the case of in-person sessions, the mediation may be held at any location that is convenient for the parties. Typically, the sessions are held at the mediator's office or in a conference room in a hotel's premises. Nothing precludes holding the mediation session at the office of one of the parties or at their lawyer's firm, provided that these locations are acceptable to both parties.

Ideally, however, the site should be neutral, so that both parties are at ease and neither feels at a disadvantage. In discussing the location, you may wish to know whether there is parking available nearby or public transportation close to the chosen site.

The setting should also be comfortable, with a table large enough to accommodate all the participants. If several persons will be attending the mediation with you and your clients, you should advise the mediator before the session to ensure that there will be enough space and seating for everyone attending the session.

There should also be two separate smaller rooms available that are acoustically isolated, so that each party and anyone accompanying them can have an area in which to privately confer with a lawyer, or where a caucus can be held.

It is preferable for there to be a flip chart or a blackboard available, so that all proposals can be readily visualized. Writing the proposals so that they are visible allows everyone to see the initial position of each party and any progress that has been made as the mediation session progresses.

Another important consideration is the availability of washrooms in the vicinity. Finally, participants appreciate the presence of coffee, tea, or juice, as well as some form of snacks. If drinks and snacks will not be provided, you may wish to find out if there is a kiosk or a store nearby where such items can be purchased.

Since not all mediators deal with lunch time in the same way, you should ask the mediator how this period will be handled. If the mediation will be continuous, you need to know whether lunch will be served or whether you and your clients are expected to bring something to eat. If a lunch break is foreseen, you may wish to inquire about what restaurants there are nearby.

In cases where your clients have a medical condition, requiring them to eat at regular intervals, it would be wise to advise the mediator of the need for breaks at certain times. You should also advise your clients to bring whatever food they will need for the duration of the mediation, as a precaution, if necessary.

## E. VIRTUAL MEDIATIONS

One case that stands out in my mind is a mediation involving a man who had sued a woman, alleging that he had lent her money over a long period for her household expenses and that she had not repaid him. The woman, in turn, claimed that the funds were a gift, not a loan, and added that they had been in a relationship.

When I questioned the parties, it became clear that they were both still struggling with the issues that had arisen between them, and they admitted that they were still interested in pursuing their relationship if these problems could be worked out. Resolving the lawsuit was not their prime concern.

At the end of the mediation, the two concluded that they would pursue couples' therapy. They embraced each other before leaving.

Why am I telling about this session? I believe that it is vitally important for the parties to be present in the same space together. The embrace at the end of the mediation session evidently could not have occurred if the mediation had taken place virtually.

Although it is preferable for the parties to deal with each other face to face, online dispute resolution has been growing rapidly.[8] Meetings in person are not always possible. Consequently, mediations by means of technology allow the process to take place. At times, virtual mediations are necessary, such as when the parties are located in different places.

Virtual mediations eliminate the inconvenience of travel, including the time and the expense involved. Often, the parties simply prefer to participate in a virtual meeting because it is more comfortable. It allows them to participate from the comfort of

---

8 Justin Monahan, "Enemy at the Gates: Online Dispute Resolution in the Time of Covid-19" *Canadian Bar Association* (16 July 2021), online: www.cba.org/Sections/Alternative-Dispute-Resolution/Resources/Resources/2021/EssayWinnerADR2021.

their own homes or offices, which may be less stressful. In addition, this option eliminates the issue of whether the mediation will take place in the office of the plaintiff's lawyer or the defendant's lawyer. Participation in an online mediation session provides a neutral meeting place for both parties.

If the mediation is held virtually, whether by Zoom, Teams, videoconferencing, or another means, mediators generally preside over the process from their offices. In the case of a settlement conference, the session is presided over by a judge, from the courthouse. Each of the parties and their lawyers can choose where they wish to be to participate in the process. You and your clients can be in separate locations. However, it is preferable for you and your clients to be in the same place so that you can easily talk to each other privately, when needed, without asking for a breakout room.

The steps followed in a virtual mediation process are the same as they are in person. On the other hand, certain factors which are specific to virtual sessions must be taken into consideration to ensure that the mediation functions properly. The following are elements to be verified before the mediation takes place:

- Ensure beforehand that you and your clients have experience with the platform chosen, whether it be Zoom, Teams, videoconference, or another means, and that your clients are comfortable with online interactions. Also ensure that if you have requested that others participate in the mediation, they are also familiar with the platform selected.
- You, your clients, or the other party may not be prepared to participate in the mediation virtually because of a lack of experience with the platform. If you are not familiar with the platform that is chosen, or your clients have never used that platform, make sure that you or your clients practice with another person beforehand, so that the mediation proceeds smoothly.
- If only one of the parties wishes to participate virtually, you may suggest to the mediator that the party who is

comfortable with virtual meetings participate online while the other party participates in person. Alternatively, if your clients are reluctant to proceed with an online mediation, inform the mediator about your clients' discomfort with this manner of proceeding and ask that the mediation session take place in person.

- Before the mediation, ensure that a link has been sent to your email and that not only the date but also the time has been established.
- Before the mediation, choose a place that provides for the best connection. Test your connection and verify that everything is in good working order.
- Verify whether the mediator will be using breakout rooms for caucusing so that, if required, you will be able to have private exchanges with your clients and with the mediator.
- Ensure that you and your clients are in an environment that is quiet. It is important that there will not be any disturbance by other people, surrounding activities, or pets during the mediation session. It is not conducive to have an animal sitting on your computer or barking during the session. It is also important not to have a third party unexpectedly enter the room.
- Tell your clients to wear an appropriate shirt or top for the mediation session. If they plan on wearing sweatpants or pyjama pants, remind them to keep such clothing out of sight.[9]
- Advise your clients to avoid multitasking during the mediation.
- Advise your clients to turn off their cellphones during the mediation so that they are not interrupted during the session.
- Adjust the screen of your clients' computer so that they can look into the camera when they are speaking.

9 Debra Bogaards, "Pants Are Optional and Forget Stilettos" *Plaintiff Magazine* (August 2020), online: https://plaintiffmagazine.com/recent-issues/item/pants-are-optional-and-forget-stilettos.

- Ensure that the camera on your computer or tablet is in a good position and that you and your clients can be seen clearly.
- Ensure that the background is appropriate. Some background choices may be too busy or distracting for a mediation session.
- Ensure that the sound level and lighting are adequate.
- Remind your clients to turn off their microphones during a break in the mediations. This will avoid any private comments being heard by the other party.
- Ensure that you have access to technical support, in case you or your clients are unable to connect with the mediator or the other party. Having technical support is also important if the connection fails during the mediation.
- If the parties become disconnected or the connection becomes faulty, determine beforehand whether an alternate means, such as the telephone, can be used to continue the mediation and, if so, ensure that you have exchanged telephone numbers with the other party and the mediator.
- Ask that the time for the mediation session be limited to a couple of hours or half a day, at the most, with adequate breaks in between. It is difficult to sit and look at a screen on a continuous basis, all day long.
- If progress is being made but the mediation is not finished, ensure that another date has been chosen to complete the mediation.
- Ensure that you have a properly working scanner to provide the mediator and the opposing party with a draft agreement if the case is settled.
- When an agreement is reached in a virtual mediation session, the agreement is usually signed virtually as well. Therefore, it is important to ensure that your clients have a functional scanner to transmit a signed copy of the agreement to the mediator and to the opposite party.
- If an agreement is reached, make sure that you follow up and obtain a copy of the agreement, signed by both parties.

## F. SCHEDULING OF MEDIATION SESSION(S)

In many cases, the mediation session only lasts a few hours or a single day, at the most. In this situation, it is often not too difficult to find a date that is convenient for all those involved in the mediation.

The length and duration of the mediation will depend on several factors, including the availability of the participants, the number of issues in dispute, the complexity of the issues, and, in some cases, the emotions involved. In certain circumstances, it may be favourable to give the parties the opportunity to consider proposals that were made during an initial session, and verify if they are feasible, before another session is held.

You should try to determine beforehand whether the mediation can be completed within a day or less. If this is not the case, you should ask the mediator to schedule several sessions at the outset.

It is preferable to set all the dates of the various sessions that will be needed to ensure that all participants will be available, particularly taking into consideration the possible demands of your clients' business or profession and the demands of your own law practice. The scheduling will obviously depend on the availability of all those who will be participating.

It is also preferable to schedule all the sessions close to each other. If too much time elapses between each meeting, not only will you lose the momentum of the process but, in addition, the parties will often try to backtrack from any progress made, making the achievement of a solution more difficult.

Finally, it is wise to ask the mediator to include the schedule of the sessions in the mediation contract.

## G. MEDIATION CONTRACT

Parties do not sign contracts in the case of settlement conferences presided by judges at the courthouse or those led by adjudicators at administrative tribunals. They simply access the settlement procedure in the manner foreseen by the jurisdiction in which they live. This ranges from a formalized request for a settlement conference, obtained by presenting a joint form to the court, to an ad hoc procedure where the time and choice of judge is sent to the trial coordinator.

In the case of private mediations, it is usual for the mediator to present a contract for the parties to sign. There is no set standard. Each mediator generally has a contract containing their own terms.

Various clauses are typically included in such a contract. Such clauses include the following:[10]

1) The identification of the parties and the mediator.
2) The preamble, containing:
    a) a summary of the elements in dispute, and
    b) the parties' declaration of their desire to settle their dispute in an amiable manner.
3) The list of elements agreed upon by the parties and the mediator, including:
    a) the voluntary nature of the process,
    b) the possibility of ending the process by the unilateral decision of one of the parties, their lawyer, or the mediator, or by reaching an agreement,
    c) the role of the mediator, and
    d) the neutrality and impartiality of the mediator.
4) The necessity for the following persons to attend the mediation:
    a) the parties to the dispute, and if they are represented by counsel, their lawyers as well,
    b) the persons who have personal knowledge of the dispute, and
    c) the persons who have the authority to settle.

---

10 The list is based on the civil and commercial mediation course offered by the bar of Quebec; other mediation organizations offer ample agreements that contain similar provisions.

5) Confidentiality:
    a) an undertaking with respect to the confidentiality of what is said, written, or done during the mediation (unless the parties subsequently have the right to use a document in the judicial process), and
    b) a renunciation of having the mediator testify in any judicial or other proceeding.
6) Caucusing: that is, the possibility for the mediator to meet separately with each party, in a caucus, whether requested by the mediator or by one of the parties or their lawyer.
7) Prescription: that is, the possibility for the parties to suspend or interrupt the delays related to prescription in their attempt to complete the process or reach an agreement.
8) Termination of the mediation: that is the possibility for the mediator to request that the parties take the necessary measures to rectify any manifest disequilibrium or injustice that exists for one of the parties and, if not, to suspend or end the mediation process.
9) Scheduling:
    a) the determination of the mediation schedule,
    b) the date that the contract must be signed, and
    c) the date that documents and/or exhibits must be remitted to the mediator.
10) Engagement of the mediator:
    a) the undertaking by the parties to retain the mediator's professional services,
    b) the undertaking by the parties to pay an equal share of the mediator's fees and expenses for the mediation (or some other percentage), including the fees for any work carried out before or after the mediation session,
    c) the undertaking to pay an advance, if so requested by the mediator, and
    d) the indication of the means of payment and when payment is to be made.
11) A stipulation that if a settlement is reached, the parties or their lawyers shall draft the agreement and any release.

Some mediators require that the contract be signed prior to the actual mediation, while others have it signed at the beginning of the first session of the mediation process. Clauses, such as those listed above, should not give rise to any disagreements.

As a lawyer, you should determine whether prescription needs to be suspended and, if so, obtain the consent of the opposite party to the suspension. In addition, you will necessarily be involved in determining the schedule of the mediation session and, if more than one session is required, the dates and times that are convenient for you and your clients.

Finally, you should review the mediation contract with your clients to ensure their acceptance of all the terms. It is advisable to point out the confidentiality aspect of the agreement. The failure to respect such a clause can potentially lead to a subsequent lawsuit.

## H. CONFIDENTIALITY AGREEMENT

There is no standard confidentiality agreement but, generally, the mediator requires that all participants in the mediation process sign a mediation protocol or agreement containing confidentiality clauses. These clauses may be drafted by the mediator or by the lawyers. The following contains an extensive list of applicable clauses:

- The parties are participating in the mediation session(s) with the intent of settling their dispute in an amicable manner.
- The parties hereto wish to keep strictly confidential all communications and documents exchanged in the mediation process.
- The parties undertake to maintain the confidentiality of all discussions held before, during, and after the mediation as well as all documents which are not already part of the court record, or which cannot otherwise be legally introduced into evidence; such discussions and documents will not be disclosed in any judicial proceeding or under any other

circumstance. Accordingly, the parties undertake not to allege, refer to, or seek to put into evidence in any proceeding, whether legal or otherwise, anything that transpires in or is related to the mediation, including any oral or written communications or any behaviour that takes place.

- The mediator, the attorneys, the parties, and any other participant in the mediation undertake to maintain the confidentiality of all aspects of the settlement discussions. They cannot be compelled to disclose the content of the discussions held, the documents exchanged, or the offers, admissions, or concessions made before, during, or after the mediation process.
- The parties recognize that they may withdraw from the mediation at any time, but they will be unable to compel the opposite party, the mediator, or any other participant to testify in any judicial or other proceeding or disclose what was said, written, or done during the mediation process.
- The parties undertake to refrain from taking any screenshots, recording in any manner, or broadcasting or transmitting the mediation process. They will not contact anyone else through any technological means, except for their lawyer, if their lawyer is not present at the mediation.

In Quebec, where parties can adopt their own rules and can contract for greater confidentiality protection than is available at common law, it is suggested that the following clause be included in the parties' agreement:

- The parties expressly contract out of the exception to settlement privilege. No disclosure whatsoever can be made in any proceeding, whether legal or otherwise, of anything that was said, written, or done in their attempt to settle their dispute, to establish the existence of an agreement, its scope, and its validity, or to establish allegations of misrepresentation, fraud, undue influence, or the bad faith of a party, or for any other purpose whatsoever.

The confidentiality agreement is signed by the parties, their lawyers, and those who will be participating in the mediation process. While some mediators provide the parties with a copy of this agreement or protocol before the mediation, typically the confidentially agreement is signed only at the beginning of the mediation session.

Settlement privilege is a rule of evidence that protects the confidentiality of all communication that takes place between parties in order to settle a conflict. Confidentiality is a fundamental aspect of the mediation process. It allows the parties to be honest and frank with each other in their discussions and allows them to express their feelings and disclose what they are really seeking, rather than their respective positions as stated in their court proceedings. The confidential nature of mediations permits the parties to communicate with each other freely, without the concern that any information exchanged, or concessions or offers made, will be used against them. Consequently, it is easier for the parties to reach an agreement.[11]

As a result of confidentiality, the parties know that, unless they authorize the mediator to inform the other party as to the information they have provided, whatever they tell the mediator will be kept in confidence. Confidentiality also allows the parties to divulge certain facts to the mediator, which will assist the mediator in bringing the parties to a settlement.

In addition, it allows the parties to express remorse or offer an apology without the fear that they will be held responsible if they do so.[12] If confidentiality were not required, parties may be inhibited from speaking freely.

Finally, the confidential nature of mediation is important if the parties settle, but it is even more important if they do not. When no agreement is reached at the end of the mediation process, the

---

11 *Union Carbide Canada Inc v Bombardier Inc*, 2014 SCC 35 at para 35.

12 Virtually all provinces in Canada now have what is known as *apology legislation*, namely legislation that protects a party from the risks of legal liability if that party offers an apology. Typically, the legislation stipulates that an apology does not constitute, in law, an express or implied admission of fault or liability.

parties will typically go to trial. If the parties were not bound by an undertaking of confidentiality when no agreement has been reached, any testimony about offers or admissions that were made or the true position of a party would place one or the other party at a clear disadvantage.

It should be noted that settlement privilege is not absolute and can be lifted to prove the existence or scope of a settlement that resulted from an agreement, as well as the purpose or validity of an agreement or the existence of fraud, misrepresentation, or bad faith.[13] Accordingly, a confidentiality clause will not prevent the production of evidence of communications in such cases, unless that is the intended effect of the mediation contract and the parties have expressly contracted for greater confidentiality.

13 *Union Carbide Canada Inc*, above note 11 at paras 34–35; *Viconte inc v Transcontinental inc*, 2020 QCCQ 1475 at paras 46–47; David Grossman, "The Limited Secrecy of Settlement Conferences (or The Truth Is Out There)" (18 May 2020), online: https://imk.ca/en/blog/limited-secrecy-settlement-conferences-truth; Peter Amrhein, "*Union Carbide Canada Inc v Bombardier Inc*: A Clarification of Privilege and Confidentiality" *CanLII Connects* (September 2015), online: https://canliiconnects.org/en/commentaries/38576; John-Paul Boyd, "Supreme Court of Canada Issues Important Judgment on Mediation, Settlements and Confidentiality" *CanLII Connects* (26 May 2014), online: https://canliiconnects.org/en/commentaries/27288. See also *Association de médiation familiale du Québec v Bouvier*, 2021 SCC 54 regarding the application of the exception to settlement privilege in the context of family mediations.

*chapter three*

# Interests and Needs of the Parties

In one of my mediation sessions, after hearing each party's version of the facts, I began asking questions about their history together. For the purposes of this discussion, I will refer to the parties as A and B.

I quickly learned that they had both immigrated to Canada and had been friends in their country of origin. In addition, their respective families were friendly with each other and often got together. A had immigrated to Canada first and had started a business. When B arrived in Canada, B joined A in a partnership.

At one point, A made a business decision without consulting B. B, who had not been informed of the decision, was insulted and hurt, and soon instituted a lawsuit against A. The lawsuit alleged that A failed to pay B in the alleged circumstances, contrary to their partnership agreement. However, the proceedings had no legal basis and only resulted because of B's hurt feelings. This was the true reason for the lawsuit.

I then asked the offending party, A, if A missed the partner's friendship. A readily agreed and, with some coaxing on my part, turned to B and expressed regret about losing B's company and friendship. B, in turn, said the same thing. A also admitted the error in having excluded B from the decision that had been made. Both parties conceded that their respective families missed their usual get-togethers and wished that the two could resolve their conflict.

The conflict was settled once the parties aired their emotions and expressed their desire to re-establish their personal relationship as well as their business relationship. The parties' interest in reconnecting with each other motivated them to end their conflict.

The concept of the parties' interests and needs is the subject of this chapter, which details the various interests that can exist in conflictual situations, and which must be considered in most mediations.

❊ ❊ ❊ ❊ ❊

Virtually all civil and commercial lawsuits conclude with a claim for money. The interests of clients are not included in the allegations because they are generally not questioned about this aspect of their conflict. In fact, lawyers rarely try to determine their clients' interests.

Unlike in a lawsuit, the interests of the parties are of utmost importance in a mediation. It is essential to identify them and deal with them if you hope to make any progress in resolving the conflict.

## A. THE CLASSIC CASE OF A CONFLICT OVER AN ORANGE

The classic example taught in introductory mediation courses is the case of two professors who are disputing the ownership of an orange in the professors' lounge.

Both professors claim they need the orange for their classroom chemistry experiment. The department head overhears the argument and tries to resolve it by suggesting that the professors cut the orange in two. However, both refuse this suggestion. This option does not satisfy either of them.

The department head can try to determine who owned the orange and who brought it into the professors' lounge. Determining who has the right to the orange constitutes the *legal* issue. However, it may not resolve the conflict since the interests of the parties can be quite different.

With appropriate questioning as to how the orange will be used, the department head learns that one professor needs the interior of the orange to observe the chemical reaction when a substance is injected into the juices of the fruit. In the other case, the professor only needs the peel since the students in that class are studying the impact of different materials on the rind.

In short, if one professor is given the inside of the orange and the other the peel, both parties will obtain what they require to satisfy their interests and needs.

On the other hand, giving the orange to only one of the professors will completely deprive the other of the experiment that was planned. Cutting the orange in two will satisfy neither of them. Finding the respective interests and needs of the parties can satisfy both.

The mediator will try to determine the interests and needs of the two parties. However, it is equally important for you, as a lawyer, to be attentive to this dimension. In fact, learning about your clients' emotions and interests may be the key to resolving the dispute or litigation. The same applies to the other party.

Parties often are angry with each other. They may have suffered aggression, disrespect, pain, humiliation, embarrassment, discouragement, jealousy, anger, frustration, or other emotions. These emotions will lead to the various interests and needs the parties may have, such as obtaining an apology, an acknowledgment of respect, or some other type of compensation, other than monetary compensation.

The conflict that developed and the parties' incapacity to resolve their differences often stem from their underlying emotions. Most often, it is necessary for the parties to express their feelings and their reactions before they can objectively deal with the facts of their case, contained in their legal proceedings.

The issues that gave rise to the conflict must be addressed for any meaningful discussion to take place and for the conflict to be resolved.

Accordingly, it is important to learn how your clients feel about the events that resulted in the conflict and what the impact was on them. It is equally important to learn about your clients' interests and needs, which, if satisfied, will reduce tensions and induce them to settle more readily.

## B. COMMON INTERESTS AND NEEDS

The interests and needs of the parties vary depending on the alleged facts involved in each case. There are, however, several specific interests that frequently arise.[1] The following interests, with examples, are amongst the most common.

### 1) Maintaining One's Reputation

Trials, with few exceptions, are open and judgments are available to the public. Occasionally, cases are reported in the media. Once liability is determined by the court and the judgment is published or reported in the media, the reputation of the losing party may well be tarnished. This is particularly the case in lawsuits involving medical or professional malpractice. Other examples include contractors whose constructions have not met required standards, service providers who have not respected their contracts or failed to provide adequate service, companies involved in the sale of goods that do not function properly, manufacturers whose products are defective, landlords renting substandard premises, employers providing unsafe working conditions, and so on. The list is extensive.

Accordingly, when a conflict arises or a lawsuit is filed, one or the other party risks having their good name sullied. Given the confidential nature of mediation, the interest in maintaining one's reputation can be a strong incentive not only to go to mediation but also to make every effort to settle the conflict.

Consider the case of a manufacturer of hardwood floors and its salesperson, who were both sued by clients after flooring was installed in their home. Soon after the installation, the clients found that their floors had warped. They instituted a lawsuit against both the manufacturer and the salesperson, seeking reimbursement for the money they

1 Most authors who write about interest-based mediation list the same or similar categories of interests. The examples used in this text are based on actual cases, but the names of the parties have been removed and since mediations are confidential, the facts have been modified sufficiently to ensure that the parties involved cannot be identified.

had paid for the flooring and the installation. The manufacturer and salesperson both denied responsibility but agreed to go to mediation.

The manufacturer was anxious to settle the case and to satisfy the customer. The company was known for serving high-end customers with custom-designed floors, and it was important for the manufacturer not to have its good reputation negatively affected. The salesperson adopted the same position.

Mediation provided the possibility of resolving the conflict without the negative publicity of a judgment.

It is important to determine how the publicity of a negative judgment can impact your clients' businesses or professional lives. The same applies to the opposing party. If your client and the other party are intent on avoiding the publicity of a trial, this information can often help the parties find common ground in a mediation session.

## 2) Preserving Confidentiality

The parties in a conflict often wish to attend a mediation to maintain the privacy of their personal lives, their financial affairs, and their business dealings. This is particularly so once they learn that not only is the outcome of a mediation confidential, but that also the discussions, offers, concessions, and documentation presented are as well (unless the documents can be produced in court). This is often the prevailing position of parties in cases involving business dealings, trade secrets, financial matters, divorce cases, and other matters of a personal nature.

Parties often have an interest in not divulging the details of their dispute. Contrary to litigation where the proceedings are accessible to the public and trials are open, mediation provides the possibility of reaching a settlement out of the public eye.

Consider the case of a sales manager of a cosmetics company who was fired. The manager sued for wrongful dismissal. The ex-employer alleged not only the manager's reduced sales levels and exaggerated expense accounts as a basis for ending the employment relationship, but also an affair the manager had with a subordinate employee during working hours, which violated company policy.

The sales manager chose to go to mediation to try to settle the case. The reasons were obvious. The manager's wife and family members were not aware of the circumstances involved in the dismissal and the manager certainly did not want them to know about the alleged personal misconduct. Mediation allowed the manager to preserve confidentiality.

When a conflict occurs or a lawsuit is instituted, what is the nature of the conflict and what are the allegations of the opposing party? It is useful to determine whether your clients or the opposite party have any personal, business, or professional information that they would want to keep confidential.

### 3) Avoiding Public Embarrassment

While confidentiality and avoiding public embarrassment may be related to each other, the desire to deal with an issue in a confidential way may have nothing to do with avoiding public embarrassment. Rather, it may simply be related to preserving the private nature of certain personal information, such as business finances.

However, when the publicity surrounding a case can bring about embarrassment for your clients, mediation is the perfect forum to avoid having the details about their conflict made public. Examples of such situations include cases concerning professional responsibility involving lawyers, notaries, dentists, doctors, accountants, engineers, architects, and brokers, among others.

The publicity surrounding the personal behaviour of an individual can also result in embarrassment when the allegations involve incompetence, mismanagement, or any type of wrongdoing, such as fraud, sexual misconduct, misrepresentation, and so on.

Similarly, public figures, such as politicians and people holding positions of prominence, will want any personal misconduct on their part to remain private, irrespective of the nature of their misconduct, particularly when they are well-known. Their behaviour is generally subject to greater scrutiny than that of the average citizen.

Even when the allegations are not proven in court, there is often a great deal of media coverage given to trials involving any type of misbehaviour, such that the person concerned has every interest in choosing mediation.

In the case cited in the previous heading, the sales manager had an interest not only in hiding the alleged misbehaviour from family members, but also in avoiding the embarrassment of having an extramarital affair made public. Mediation provided the privacy that was needed.

### 4) Not Creating a Precedent

There are situations when a company that is sued wishes to resolve a conflict quickly and quietly and, most importantly, in a way that does not set a precedent for other similar cases that can arise.

This may occur in cases where the plaintiffs allege that a company's negligence, errors, or defective products resulted in damage. A judgment rendered on such issues against a company, institution, or organization will set the stage for the next case, and could become a dangerous precedent for those involved.

Consider the personal injury lawsuit filed in Pennsylvania, United States, against Amazon regarding product liability. A woman bought a dog collar on Amazon from a third-party seller. When walking her dog, the dog collar broke, hit her in the left eye, and resulted in a permanent loss of vision in her eye. She filed a lawsuit against Amazon. The company denied responsibility, claiming it was not the seller. The District Court rendered judgment in favour of Amazon, but the woman appealed the judgment. The Third US Circuit Court of Appeals held that Amazon was responsible for consumer injuries caused by defective products purchased on amazon.com.[2] The case was appealed to the Pennsylvania Supreme Court, but the parties came to an agreement before that court could decide the issue. Amazon settled the

2 *Oberdorf v Amazon.com Inc*, 2019 No 18-1041 (3d Cir); Eric T. Chaffin, "Amazon Skirts Potential Liability Precedent by Settling Personal Injury Case" (28 September 2020), online: https://newyork.legalexaminer.com/legal/amazon-skirts-potential-liability-precedent-by-settling-personal-injury-case.

case to avoid a precedent that could be potentially dangerous. If the court ruled in favour of the victim, it would have been more difficult for Amazon to maintain its lack of liability in other cases involving defective products.

It is important for you to be aware of the possibility that a situation could create a precedent, either for your clients or for the opposite party. In either case, the avoidance of a precedent will be an inducement for the impacted party to participate in mediation and reach a settlement.

### 5) Being Heard and Understood

Both parties have an interest in being heard and understood.

Complainants or plaintiffs who have suffered material, physical, or moral damage believe they have been wronged and seek compensation. They have a story to tell and issues they want to address. The mediation may be the first time they have had an opportunity to relate their version of the facts to a neutral person, namely the mediator, and possibly even to the other party.

The opposite parties, when sued, usually consider that they have done nothing wrong and are not responsible; rather, they believe that the plaintiffs or complainants are at fault, or, in some cases, that a third party is responsible.

The defendants also have a story to tell and will welcome the opportunity to provide their version of the facts. In some cases, they have been negatively impacted by the behaviour of the complainants or plaintiffs and need a venue to express their position and feelings. Sometimes, it is the very first time that anyone has considered their side of the story.

Consider a dispute between the director of a hospital's financial department and a doctor carrying out research. According to the established rules, the hospital's approval was required for the purchase of any equipment. Generally, it took several weeks before authorization was granted. Because of the delay, rather than following these rules, the doctor bought the equipment that was needed for various research projects before obtaining the requisite approval, and then demanded reimbursement from the hospital. When the hospital refused, the doctor sued both the hospital and the financial director for the cost of the equipment.

The doctor explained that if it was necessary to wait until the director of the financial department gave the necessary approval, too much time would elapse and the grant funds would be depleted, because the researchers were still being paid while waiting for the equipment to arrive. The doctor's story was compelling, but the hospital's financial director also had a story to tell.

The financial director explained that the financial department was responsible for the financial requests of over a hundred doctors and research heads. There was a procedure to follow, and all the staff respected it except for this doctor. The doctor's behaviour caused the financial director continued administrative and accounting problems that were exceedingly difficult to resolve, and regularly required all the members of the financial department to do extra work.

The financial director had previously refunded the money that the doctor had spent on research equipment without authorization. However, the ongoing problem caused so much frustration that the director ultimately refused to reimburse the doctor for any subsequent purchases. When the doctor repeated the behaviour anyway, the financial director refused to authorize the reimbursement, and the lawsuit was born.

While the doctor's situation was widely known, the mediation was the first time the financial director had a chance to explain the impact that the doctor's behaviour had on the financial department. It was also the first time the doctor in question would hear about the director's plight. In short, the financial director had not simply adopted an obstinate position for the sake of meaningless red tape. There were real administrative implications. The director needed to express them, be heard, and be understood.

More importantly, the explanations each party provided, which the other party heard for the first time, allowed them to discuss the problem and find a means for the doctor to access the equipment that was truly needed within a more rapid timeframe. They also provided a means for administrating this variation of procedure in such a way that did not negatively impact the hospital's financial administration.

### 6) Obtaining an Explanation

A lawsuit is generally instituted because one party has been affected by the other party's actions or words. Very often, there has never been the opportunity to find out the reason behind the opposing party's behaviour or statements. Frequently, parties only hear an explanation long after the incident occurred. Moreover, in a trial, the aggrieved parties may never get an explanation that would make a difference in their attitude toward the opposite party.

Mediation provides the opportunity for each party to hear the other party's version of what led to the conflict and their perspective of the case. They may get to the root of the conflict for the very first time.

Consider the case of a company that contracted with a well-known TV host to use the host's image on the company's vehicles as publicity for its product in return for a set amount of compensation. The contract was for a specific duration. However, at its expiry, the company failed to remove the image from its vehicles.

The TV host demanded the image be removed, and when that did not occur, the host sued for damages. The host no longer wanted the image associated with the company's business and also wanted to know why the company had not proceeded to remove this photo from all the company's vehicles.

A trial would concentrate on the company's failure to respect the parties' contract and would deal with the amount of damages claimed. But the TV host also had an interest in obtaining an explanation from the company. Mediation allowed for a frank discussion of the issue and for the TV host to obtain an explanation.

As it turned out, the delay in removing the image of the TV host from the company's vehicles was not due to the company's bad faith or its intention to profit from a breach of contract. Rather, the company had failed to repaint all its vehicles because of financial difficulties. Mediation allowed the TV host to learn the reason for the lengthy delay in having the host's image removed from the company's vehicles. The explanation led the parties to work out a timetable for the required paint job as well as a compensation plan, and ultimately reach an agreement.

## 7) Obtaining Acknowledgement or Respect

A person's credibility, reliability, honesty, or competence may have been challenged by the opposite party. In such cases, the affected individual will seek to regain the respect of the opposite party and some acknowledgement that the facts presented by the opposing party are not valid.

A case in point is that of a professional photographer who sued a children's dance school. The school hired the photographer to take photos of the children, but then the photographer did not receive any orders from their parents. This was a marked difference from previous years, when the photographer received multiple orders.

The photographer claimed that the school had not shown the proofs to the children's parents. According to the lawsuit, if the parents had seen the photographs, the photographer would have received the usual number of annual orders.

The school had denied the claim in the legal proceedings and maintained that the photographs were of poor quality. However, in mediation, the school's representative acknowledged its omission in handling the matter and undertook to try to rectify the situation.

This admission readily brought about a settlement between the parties. The photographer, in this case, not only had a need to have the photographs distributed to the parents in question and obtain orders, but also needed to establish that the school's claims were unfounded. Although the photographer wanted the business, more important for the photographer was the need for the school's administration to acknowledge the photographer's competence and quality work.

## 8) Obtaining an Apology or Expression of Regret

A lawsuit will set out the alleged facts and the remedy sought, which is usually monetary compensation. In mediation, complainants or plaintiffs also seek monetary compensation. However, an apology can play a large role in bringing about a settlement.

Often, what drives the anger or hostility toward the opposite party is the hurt felt by the complainants or plaintiffs, who feel that they were treated badly, wrongly, or abusively. The party who has been affected needs to hear some recognition that the alleged behaviour was inappropriate in order to move on.

If the opposing party is willing to apologize or, at the very least, express their regret about what transpired, it often helps the complainants or plaintiffs put the past behind them and have a reasonable discussion to try to settle the dispute.

Frequently, the party who is prepared to apologize fails to do so for fear of incurring legal responsibility. In most jurisdictions, apology legislation has been adopted such that an apology is no longer seen as the basis for litigation. Although it no longer constitutes an admission of fault or evidence to establish liability in a lawsuit, it nevertheless is often interpreted as such by the wrongdoer.

Apologies can be significant in resolving conflict. The power of an apology lies in the acknowledgement of remorse and the admission of responsibility. An apology, as an expression of remorse, has been found to have a calming effect and the power to heal a broken or damaged relationship, since it satisfies a need on the part of the recipients to hear the opposing party acknowledge that they made a mistake or that the responsible party is assuming responsibility for the wrongdoing.[3]

Consider the case of an investment broker who accepted funds from a client and lost virtually all the assets, despite the fact that the client,

---

3 Brian Curial & Maria Chau, "I'm Sorry (Please Don't Sue Me)," online: www.millerthomson.com/assets/files/article_attachments/Please%20Don't%20Sue%20Me.pdf; Marc Horsburgh, "The Power of an Apology" (29 January 2023), online: www.theglobeandmail.com/life/first-person/article-i-needed-my-doctor-to-apologize-before-i-could-let-go-of-my-trauma.

who was averse to a high level of risk, had informed the broker of this fact. The client not only sought some amount of compensation, but also sought an apology from the investment broker.

The investment broker had not intentionally made poor investment choices and wished to express concern for the client's situation without admitting responsibility.

In mediation, the broker ultimately expressed regrets that the client's investment portfolio had not performed as well as expected, and assured the client that the outcome was unintended.

Although the broker did not specifically state *I apologize for what I did*, the words were acceptable to meet the complainant's need for an apology.

## 9) Re-establishing a Relationship

In virtually every instance when a dispute arises, a relationship that had existed ends for the people involved. The parties may never want to see each other again because of their distrust of each other and their mutual hostility.

There are cases concerning a business relationship, a family relationship, or a friendship where the parties previously had a strong bond and would genuinely like to re-establish the relationship they had, if their conflict can be resolved. However, it is most unusual for a previous relationship to be re-established when the parties go to trial. In court, which takes place in an adversarial system, only the negative aspects of the dispute will be aired.

In mediation, on the other hand, various techniques can be used that will defuse the hostility and anger and allow each party to see the other's perspective. Once the core reasons for the conflict are identified, explanations can be provided and emotions expressed. It then becomes possible to consider how to reach an agreement that may include, as an option, the re-establishment of the parties' relationship.

Consider the case of man who sued his two daughters and their spouses over a country house that had been gifted to them. The father wanted to annul the gift. He did not speak to his daughters and their spouses for several years because of their conflict. Despite their reticence, they all agreed to attend a mediation session.

During the mediation, the father told his adult children that he had never intended to give up the country house, but his late wife, their mother, had forced him to carry out the transfer. When he asked his daughters and their spouses to return the property, they refused, explaining that they had carried out extensive renovations, which had been very costly.

The daughters and their spouses were not aware that their father had been opposed to the gift of the country house and consequently couldn't understand their father's demand that it be given back. They only learned of their mother's behaviour during the mediation. At the same time, they all admitted that the transfer of the country house had torn their family apart and they all missed the closeness they once had.

While they understood their father's desire to take back the ownership of the country house, they pointed to the fact that they had invested a considerable amount of money in the property.

After fruitful discussions, the parties agreed that the father would contribute to the cost of the renovations, and as a counterpart, his daughters and their spouses would allow him ongoing use of the country house, with the choice of using it on alternating weekends or sharing the premises with them.

This settlement came about, in large part, because of the parties' interest in re-establishing the family relationship.

### 10) Allowing Future Business Relations

When a dispute arises between two parties with a business relationship, the relationship is often ended. However, the parties may have an interest in having a future relationship if they are able to successfully deal with their conflict. Mediation, rather than litigation, allows for the possibility of such a relationship to take place once the conflict is resolved.

Consider the case of two people who had a contractual relationship that fell apart. One had a company that collected cooking oil from a restaurant, paying for the oil and reselling it afterwards, for a profit. Obtaining the oil at a good price was beneficial for the company. The owner of the restaurant needed to dispose of the oil after it was used in the cooking process. Having an outlet for the disposal of the oil was beneficial for the restaurant.

A problem arose over the application of the terms of their contract with each other. The company was paying less for the oil than the restaurant owner believed they had agreed upon.

Angry about the company's position, the restaurant stopped supplying its oil to the company. The two stopped dealing with each other, and the company, which was no longer obtaining any oil, sued the restaurant, alleging a breach of contract.

The parties agreed to mediation. Their conflict clearly resulted from the ambiguous terms of their contract. However, both recognized that a good working relationship was a plus. As a result, the parties agreed that they could continue to work together if they both had the same understanding of the terms of the contract governing their business relationship. This led to an agreement to work out new terms of their contract and to jointly choose a lawyer who would redraft the contract.

Mediation allowed the parties to re-establish their business relationship — one that would work for both parties.

### 11) Ending the Conflict Quickly

For some, the stress, time, and the cost involved in a lawsuit are overwhelming, and the parties wish to end the process as soon as possible. They frequently opt for mediation, since it is a means of putting an end to the conflict long before their case is scheduled for trial.

Litigants who do not want to go to court will not only accept mediation as a means of resolving a dispute but will also not be overly aggressive in negotiating the best outcome. This interest in quickly ending the dispute will generally lead to a rapid settlement, although frequently parties who clearly wish to avoid a trial will settle for less than what they originally hoped to obtain as plaintiffs, or will settle by paying more than originally intended, in the case of defendants.

A case that demonstrates this is that of a person who sold a cleaning business to a colleague. In addition to the purchase price, the seller was to receive the payment of a set sum of money each time the purchaser serviced a previous client.

The seller claimed that the defendant, namely the purchaser, had failed to properly pay the amounts agreed upon, pursuant to the contract the parties had concluded, and instituted a lawsuit.

However, the seller was not in good health and the stress of facing a trial was making the seller's illness worse. The situation was having a negative impact on the seller's well being. Unable to deal with the ongoing stress any longer, the seller clearly had an interest in settling the lawsuit as quickly as possible.

The defendant was a hardnosed opponent. The offer the defendant presented was not nearly as much as the seller expected or had sought at the outset of the mediation, but given the seller's concerns and the interest in settling the litigation as quickly as possible, the seller accepted the defendant's offer.

In cases such as the one described above, mediation allows for the rapid resolution of the conflict and the removal of ongoing stress. However, in such situations, it is important to protect your clients and ensure that the other party does not take advantage of them. This can be done in a caucus, where you can privately offer advice to your clients during the mediation session, counselling your clients not to offer too much (if they are the defendants) or not to accept an unreasonable amount (if they are the plaintiffs).

### 12) Financial Interest

Clearly, complainants or plaintiffs have an interest in obtaining compensation from the other party. However, there is always a risk in going to court. The outcome is never certain. The plaintiffs' cases can be dismissed, or they may obtain judgment in their favour but be awarded only a small portion of what they were seeking.

There is a risk involved for the defendants or recipients of a complaint, as well. They may be ordered to pay if not the entire amount of the claim, then a substantial amount, in addition to legal fees and court costs.

In the case of a company, the cost of a lengthy and expensive trial often has implications for many people and not simply one individual. The considerations include the amount budgeted for potential claims, the problems involved in future cash flow issues, and the financial impact of a lawsuit on the company's shareholders.

Mediation offers the possibility of alternatives that are significantly less costly. For example, in the case of a defective product, a company could offer the plaintiff new equipment as a replacement. The cost to the company, which manufactures the product, would be less than paying the defendant a sufficient amount to purchase the equipment elsewhere.

It is also in the plaintiffs' interest to settle and to be ensured of immediately obtaining some amount of compensation following a settlement, rather than having to wait for a judgment to be rendered.

In short, while each party has a different view as to the amount payable, both parties have an interest in agreeing upon a mutually satisfactory monetary amount. Such a result can be achieved in mediation.

### 13) Other Interests

Some mediators list other interests which are related to specific areas of conflict, such as consumer litigation, medical responsibility, or harassment conflicts.

In the area of consumer litigation, for example, when a product has been found to be defective, consumers may have an interest in obtaining a replacement product. Alternatively, the consumers' interest will be in having the product repaired by the company or obtaining compensation so that they can have it repaired on their own. The business in question will have a desire for confidentiality, particularly if, after testing, the defect has been detected in many of that specific model. It will also have an interest in avoiding the possibility of a class action instituted against it.

In the area of medical responsibility, patients who allege that the follow-up period after their diagnosis was too short and whose illness has recurred may be interested in having the screening policy changed so that others are not exposed to similar shortcomings. The hospital will want to avoid any publicity about the issue while the treating physician may have an interest in establishing that the current screening policy conforms to existing medical standards. The doctor will also have an interest in maintaining a good reputation.

Harassment complaints in the workplace also result in specific interests. When such a complaint is filed by employees against their supervisors, the employees may have an interest in bringing to light abusive behaviour so that they are no longer subjected to the harassment. Alternatively, the employees may have an interest in moving from the department where they are working to another department, in order to avoid any contact with the supervisors. The supervisors, on the other hand, may have an interest in clearing their names. From the perspective of the company, it has an interest in avoiding a lawsuit as well as the negative publicity associated with it.

Different kinds of conflicts will elicit different interests. Consequently, it is important to look for the interests and needs that could satisfy your clients and be instrumental in bringing about a settlement.

## C. THE CHOICE OF A TRIAL

In some cases, instead of attempting to resolve the conflict amiably, the interests of the parties induce them to seek their *day in court*. In cases of medical malpractice, for example, victims may wish to go to court, rather than settle, to expose what they consider as incompetence on the part of a doctor and prevent similar errors from occurring in the future.

In consumer cases, the consumer may want a trial to publicly expose a company and have it publicly reprimanded. In commercial conflicts, a company may choose to have a trial so that it can defend a principle that is important to it. It might also opt for a trial where a favourable judgment will be to the company's advantage. The choice of a trial rather than mediation may be influenced by a decision of the board of directors or pressure from shareholders.

In cases of harassment in a workplace, if the accused is a manager, the accused may want a trial to obtain a judgment that officially recognizes the absence of inappropriate behaviour. Similarly, the complainant may want a trial to publicly expose the behaviour and ensure that no one else is exposed to similar harassment in the future.

❊ ❊ ❊ ❊ ❊

The above-mentioned reasons for choosing a trial over mediation are not commonplace. Most parties are amenable to mediation or another type of dispute resolution once the nature of the process and its advantages are explained.[4] The various interests listed in this chapter are common and are often what induce parties to opt for a means of settling their conflict, rather than go to court.

In summary, irrespective of the conflict, and despite the claim set out in a demand letter or legal proceedings, which virtually always involves financial compensation, a monetary settlement is not always the actual result sought. Often, the interests of the parties, such as those described above, are as important if not more important than the financial compensation that may be obtained. In many cases, once the origin of the conflict is discovered and the interests of the parties are met, the parties more easily come to a resolution, with or without financial compensation.

---

4 While mediation is common in family conflicts, one of the exceptions to participating in a mediation occurs when a party is a victim of domestic abuse. In such a case, mediation is rarely the forum chosen.

The issue of interests of clients is typically overlooked in lawsuits. However, their importance in mediation cannot be overemphasized. It is essential to discuss this question with your clients when you prepare to go to mediation. As already indicated, it may well be the key to the success of reaching a settlement.

*chapter four*

# Preparing for Mediation

In many of the mediations over which I have presided, problems arose simply because the lawyers had not prepared for the mediation and had not prepared their clients to participate in the process.

There were occasions when a lawyer would arrive with a representative from a company or an organization who did not know the facts of the case or did not have the authority to make a final decision. At times, one of the lawyers arrived with a client who did not fully comprehend the English language, but the lawyer had not considered the services of an interpreter. In other instances, after explaining how the process would proceed and hearing the parties explain how the conflict arose, the parties would sit back and expect me to render a decision, which of course is not the role of the mediator. In still other cases, the lawyers based their clients' position on the conclusions of their lawsuits and had not discussed with their clients what compromises they were prepared to make to reach a settlement or what their bottom line was. Just as important, clients were often not aware of the weaknesses in their case or the risks involved in going to court if they did not settle.

Some of these issues can be resolved at the mediation, such as providing the parties with the explanations that the lawyers had failed to provide. However, in other situations, the lack of preparation may lead to a breakdown in the negotiations or even constitute an impediment for the mediation taking place. Consequently, the importance of preparing for a mediation cannot be emphasized enough.

This chapter deals with the decisions that you need to make and the discussions that need to take place prior to the mediation session.

## A. INTRODUCTION

At this point, several decisions have been made. You have already:

- Discussed with your clients the nature of the mediation process and its advantages.
- Convinced your clients, in a jurisdiction where mediation is voluntary, to participate in a mediation session.
- Contacted the lawyer of the opposing party, and the other party has agreed to participate in the process.
- Discussed the choice of a mediator with your clients.
- Selected a mediator in conjunction with the opposite party.
- Contacted the mediator to schedule the mediation.
- Determined whether the mediation will be virtual or in person and, if in person, established the location where it will take place.
- Discussed your clients' availability on various dates when the mediation session(s) can be held and established the date(s) with the mediator and the other party.
- Given your clients a copy of the mediation contract for their signature and obtained a signed copy.

There will still be several other decisions to be made before attending the mediation session.

Mediation is an informal process and is not a trial. This does not mean that no preparation is required. On the contrary, to be effective counsel for your clients, it is important that you prepare for the mediation and that you prepare your clients as well.

While the mediator is responsible for the process and will review the material provided by the parties before the mediation, you, as a lawyer, will carry out the necessary work to ensure that the session is cooperative and productive. Your preparation involves your documentation, the explanations you give to your clients, the presentation(s) you and your clients will be making, and your strategy.

Preparation involves not only explaining the process to your clients and preparing them to assume their role in the mediation, but also considering the many other decisions that must be made, including who will be present at the mediation, how the facts will be presented, the order of subjects to be discussed, your negotiation strategy, your client's proposals for settlement, what non-monetary options can be suggested, and so on.

In this section, we will consider the topics that you will deal with, the decisions you will make, and the actions you will take before the actual mediation begins.

The following is a useful checklist. Each of the items will be more fully detailed below:

1) Consider when to prepare your clients for the mediation session.
2) Describe the nature and the objectives of mediation.
3) Describe the steps of the process.
4) Explain the role of each participant.
5) Describe what will take place.
6) Discuss how to dress.
7) Determine the participants in the mediation.
8) Identify any language barriers.
9) Identify any cultural issues.
10) Discuss the strengths and weaknesses of the case.
11) Identify the interests and needs of the parties.
12) Prepare the documents and facts needed.
13) Prepare a brief.
14) Prepare your clients to present the facts.
15) Prepare your clients to discuss emotions.
16) Carry out a mock presentation.
17) Discuss what your clients are willing to offer or accept.
18) Think outside the box and consider non-monetary options.
19) Discuss strategy with your clients, including:
    a) any non-starters,
    b) the order of subjects to discuss,

   c) the use of caucuses, and
   d) the pace of the proposals.

20) Determine your clients' bottom line.
21) Discuss your clients' Best Alternative To a Negotiated Agreement (BATNA), as well as their best-case and worst-case scenarios.
22) Discuss the costs of not settling.

## B. TOPICS TO CONSIDER AND DEAL WITH

### 1) Consider When to Prepare Your Clients for the Mediation Session

You want your clients to be ready for the mediation session. There is no fixed time when you must meet, but your advice and preparation should be fresh in your clients' minds on the day of the mediation. Therefore, your preparation should take place close to the date of the session, within approximately five days. However, it should not be immediately before the session. You should leave time to meet again, in case your clients are not fully prepared after the first meeting.

### 2) Describe the Nature and Objectives of Mediation

Most often, your clients have never been to a mediation session. It may be as stressful to them as a trial. Therefore, there are several aspects to the process that you should explain to your clients so that they understand what mediation entails:

- Describe the nature of the process as being akin to negotiating with the opposite party with the assistance of a neutral third party, namely the mediator.
- Advise your clients that the process is not formal. The mediator will not be wearing robes and you, as a lawyer, will not wear a robe either.
- Tell your clients where the mediation will take place if it will be in person.
- If the mediation will be held virtually, arrange for your clients to be present with you.

- Ensure that your clients will be available on the date or dates scheduled.
- Make sure that your clients will be present for the entire duration of the scheduled mediation to avoid ending the session prematurely, without an agreement.
- Discuss the objectives of the mediation and remind your clients that they are not there to win or to establish that their case is well-founded but to reach a satisfactory solution to their conflict, and that to do so, there must be some give and take.

### 3) Describe the Steps of the Process

Mediation is less formal than a trial and there are generally few rules, other than the requirement to be civil and to listen when the other party is speaking. While mediators' strategies differ and there are differences in approach and technique, experienced mediators tend to employ similar practices. The usual process comprises different steps, which can be described as follows:

- Introduction and explanation of the process by the mediator.
- Presentation of the facts by each party.
- Exploration of the parties' interests and needs.
- Determination and negotiation of options for a solution.
- Selection of the option(s) for settlement.
- Drafting of the agreement.

Some mediators include another step at the beginning and ask the parties to describe how their relationship began and what was positive about it.

It is useful for you to understand not only how the mediation proceeds but also the importance of following through with each step. Frequently, lawyers arrive at a mediation session and attempt to modify the process at the outset by stating that they wish to begin with the negotiations.

However, experience has shown that the parties must be allowed to talk about their version of the facts and their perspective as to what led to the conflict. If the parties have not had the opportunity to fully explain their position to each other as well as express their emotions, an impasse will often occur. The parties will typically return to relating the facts that underlie their positions, as they perceive them, and the possibility of a settlement then becomes minimal.

### 4) Explain the Role of Each Participant

The mediator will:

- Act as a neutral and impartial person.
- Control the process and act as *an orchestra leader*.
- Facilitate communication between the parties.
- Assist the parties to determine options that are acceptable to them.
- Help the parties negotiate possible proposals for a settlement.
- Encourage the parties to be imaginative in finding solutions.
- Perhaps meet separately with each of the parties to determine how a settlement can be reached.
- *Not* issue orders.
- *Not* determine the outcome of the conflict, impose a solution on the parties, or render a decision.
- *Not* give an opinion or offer a solution (unless they have been engaged as an evaluative mediator).
- *Not* be called upon to testify subsequently as to what transpired during the mediation session(s).

The parties must:

- Be present at the mediation session (either in person or virtually).
- Be committed to try to settle their dispute.
- Have the authority to settle or readily be able to obtain this authority.
- Have the occasion to present their story as well as their emotions and must be prepared to do so.

- Be prepared to actively participate in the mediation session with an open mind and a willingness to compromise.
- Be willing to listen.
- Be flexible and prepared to modify their positions and explore options.
- Negotiate in good faith.
- Give their consent freely to any settlement reached.
- Sign the agreement reached.
- Respect the confidentiality of the process.
- Respect the conclusion reached if there is a settlement.

The lawyers will:

- Explain the mediation process to their clients.
- Determine their clients' interests and needs.
- Prepare a statement of the issues in dispute, if required.
- Prepare their clients to present their stories and their emotions.
- Prepare their clients to participate effectively in the mediation process.
- Assist their clients in negotiating and in evaluating the proposals put forward.
- Suggest caucuses when needed.
- Assist in overcoming impasses.
- Re-evaluate their clients' position, if necessary.
- Provide ongoing strategic and legal advice.
- Protect their clients' legal interests with respect to any agreement their clients may wish to make.
- Draft or participate in drafting the agreement if a settlement is reached.
- Collaborate with the mediator throughout the process.

## 5) Describe What Will Take Place

After reviewing the process with your clients, advise them that they will begin by making an opening statement (that you will prepare with them). Advise your clients that, contrary to court proceedings, you will not be questioning them or the other party; rather, your clients will be presenting their version of the facts and the other party will also present their version of the facts.

Assure your clients that while you will not be questioning the other party, you will nevertheless be present to help them participate in all the aspects of the mediation. Inform them that both parties and their lawyers will participate in an initial plenary session to discuss possible options for a settlement.

Explain the use of the caucus— that is, the situation where you and your clients have the possibility of meeting with the mediator to confidentially discuss any aspect of the case, in the absence of the other party. The mediator can request a caucus or you, as counsel, can request one.

Advise your clients that, with your help, they will be negotiating with the opposing party, and the mediation will take place in a plenary session, or in caucuses, or in both. Explain that they must actively participate in the mediation and negotiate in good faith. Inform them that if they reach a settlement with the other party, you or together with the other lawyer will draft the agreement, and that they must sign the agreement.

Advise your clients of the confidential nature of the process, namely that nothing said or written during the mediation process can be divulged in any circumstances, after the mediation. Make sure your clients understand that they must respect the conditions of the settlement. They must understand that they may not speak about any of the information obtained during the mediation or the outcome of the mediation. The divulgation of such information violates any undertaking they will make and can potentially have legal consequences.

### 6) How to Dress for the Mediation

What is worn at a mediation is important. Often, how one dresses is the first means of communication. It reveals information about the person and provides the mediator and the participants with a first overall impression. While mediation is not as formal a process as a trial, at the same time, it is not a casual event. Most advisers suggest that the attire for a mediation session should be in-between a very formal look and a casual one and refer to the appropriate dress as *business casual*.[1]

It is important that the clothing that is worn or one's appearance does not distract from the mediation and the discussions that take place. Consequently, *less is more*. It is advisable for your clients to select a simple look in dark or neutral colours, preferably solids rather than wild patterns, and wear reasonable or simple accessories. They should dress in clothing that is comfortable but also makes them feel good about themselves, providing them with a sense of confidence.

Advise your clients to avoid wearing anything that is outlandish, provocative, or distracting, such as T-shirts with inflammatory wording on them, flashy accessories and footwear, or glitzy jewellery.[2] It is also recommended that your clients have a hair trim before the mediation session.

Although you should advise your clients as to how to dress, it is also important for you to consider what you will wear to the mediation. Some consider that dressing very formally is appropriate to establish your authority, while others believe that somewhat informal clothing is more conducive to making people feel more relaxed and open to communicating.[3]

In choosing what you will wear, consider who the mediator and who your opponent will be and what their style is. You should

---

1 Carolyn Woodruff, "Mediation Fashion, Accessories, Planning, and Food" *Ask Carolyn* (26 January 2022), online: www.askcarolyn.co/mediation-fashion-accessories-planning-and-food; *Her Lawyer*, "What Should Women Wear to Divorce Mediation?" (11 July 2021), online: https://herlawyer.com/what-women-wear-mediation.

2 Whitley Adkins, "What to Wear: Your Style Guide for Mediation + Court" *Clair Samuel's Law Blog* (26 January 2021), online: https://clairesamuelslaw.com/blog/how-to-dress.

3 David Ross, "Polo Shirts, Power Ties and Pant Suits: Strategic Clothing Choices for Virtual Mediations" *JAMS-ADR Insights* (21 September 2020), online: www.jamsadr.com/blog/2020/polo-shirts-power-ties-and-pant-suits-strategic-clothing-choices-for-virtual-mediations.

dress respectfully, being mindful that what you wear will send signals to the mediator and the participants. Accordingly, in some mediations a Rolex watch is entirely appropriate, while in others, it would be best to leave it at home. Similarly, some participants are comfortable with a more informal attire while others may feel disrespected if you do not dress formally. Therefore, before reaching for any outfit, consider how you will present yourself and what information you will be conveying by what you wear.

### 7) Determine the Participants in the Mediation

#### a) The Party to the Proceedings

It might seem obvious that both parties to a conflict must be present at the mediation. However, on occasion, lawyers decide that since they have a mandate to represent their clients, they can attend the mediation on behalf of their clients. This approach is not recommended.

It is most important for your clients to be present at the mediation session, either in person or virtually. Otherwise, who will explain their emotions and feelings? Who will express their interests? How will they understand the perspective of the other party? How will they be able to see what progress or concessions have been made? How can they provide their consent to any agreement reached if they were not present during the negotiations and are not fully aware of what transpired?

To have a successful outcome, your clients' presence and active participation is essential.

#### b) The Person Aware of the Facts

It is essential that the party present at the mediation includes a person who is personally aware of the facts. Occasionally, a company will send a representative to the mediation who has no knowledge of the conflict or perhaps was not even working at the company at the time the conflict took place.

However, it is most difficult for a participant who was not involved in the conflict to accurately describe what occurred, refute the version of the other party, and provide their own perspective. It is essential that an individual who does have such knowledge be present as well.

### c) The Person with the Authority to Settle

Most often, both parties to a conflict are aware of the facts and they also have the authority to settle. However, this is not always the case.

There are many instances when the persons who are present and who know the facts do not have full authority to decide or to settle the case. This is particularly true in the case of companies where a representative participates in the mediation, but a superior, a manager, an officer, or the board of directors as a whole will ultimately determine the monetary and non-monetary conditions that are acceptable to resolve the dispute.

If the persons with the authority to settle are not present, how will they comprehend the evolution of the parties' positions and the offers that have taken place over time? If they had adopted a firm position before the mediation, how will they understand the impact of new information or new perspectives that have emerged? How can they accept a particular outcome if they were given one set of information before the mediation but have not followed the progression of the negotiations, which led to the proposed solution? How will the true deciders be convinced that the proposed solution is the best possible if they have not participated in the evolution of the negotiations?

Because of these issues, it is essential to ensure that those who are the actual decision-makers in the process will be present or, at the very least, will participate through technological means and keep abreast of the ongoing negotiations at each step of the way.

In certain circumstances, a proposed settlement can be transmitted by telephone, email, or text to the person or persons deciding the mediation. However, unless the proposed outcome is only slightly different from what had been adopted as the party's stand before the mediation, or unless the contact has been continuous with respect to the evolution of the proposals and the negotiations, it is unlikely that the proposed settlement will be accepted.

Therefore, you must make sure that your clients have the authority to settle or can be in ongoing contact with the person or persons who will be determining whether or not a final proposal is acceptable. Since many, if not most, mediations now take place virtually, it is not difficult for the decision-maker to watch the process. In the case where a board of directors will make the decision, it would be too cumbersome for all the board members to participate in the mediation. However, it is important for at least one member to be present, with a mandate from the board to decide on behalf of the other members.

It is not only important that those persons with authority are present or are following the negotiations, but it is also important to have such assurance beforehand. Imagine that after a lengthy and emotional mediation, the parties reach an agreement, but then, at the last minute, the opposing party and counsel advise you that they cannot provide the necessary consent but must obtain authorization from someone at a higher level in the organization or from their partners. The settlement at that point may well unravel.

### d) An Expert Witness

You may wish to have an expert present at the mediation. If so, you should discuss this option first with the mediator. If you have asked an expert to be present without first obtaining the mediator's consent, and your expert is not permitted to remain at the mediation, your clients will have incurred an unnecessary expense. However, in the case where the mediator agrees with your request, you must advise the lawyer representing the other party so that they can invite an expert to attend as well, if they so wish.

Certain mediators welcome the presence of experts. They can be helpful in explaining complex technical issues and in jointly presenting solutions for settlement. However, others prefer that only the parties participate in the process, particularly in the classic cases of mediation. The presence of experts with conflicting opinions may not be conducive to a collaborative resolution. It is important to remember that in interest-based mediation, mediators do not provide an evaluation of the case and the purpose is not to determine responsibility; rather, the goal is to resolve the conflict by meeting the parties' interests and needs. Therefore, in most cases, an expert is not needed.

#### e) An Insurance Representative and the Insured

Cases involving insurance companies are another example of situations where the person who has personal knowledge of the facts and the person making the decision are not the same.

In cases of civil responsibility, such as a malpractice lawsuit, the insurance company is often responsible for its insured's liability. The insurance company will be subrogated in the rights of its insured client and will act on behalf of the client. In such cases, a representative from the insurance company must be present, since the representative will be the one determining how much will be paid to the other party.

Even when a representative of the insurance company is present, the insured should also be present at the mediation, whether or not the insured's consent is required. The insured, generally, is the one who is aware of the facts of the case, not the insurance representative, and will be able to provide whatever information is necessary.

The insured can also play a role in expressing their feelings and perspective on the case. This person is also involved in the litigation and has an interest in the negotiations that take place in the mediation as well as the outcome. In particular, the insured has a vested interest in resolving the dispute in cases of professional responsibility.

### 8) Identify Any Language Barriers

It is necessary to consider, prior to the mediation, any language issues that will arise. If your clients do not understand English (or the language in which the mediation takes place) and will have difficulty either comprehending what is said or expressing themselves during the mediation, you should advise the mediator of this fact. If the two parties do not share a native tongue, it is possible that a linguistic nuance may have been the cause of a misunderstanding and ultimately the cause of their conflict.

If that is the case, or in cases where your clients will have difficulty expressing themselves in the language in which the mediation takes place, consider hiring an interpreter. The use of an interpreter usually results in more cumbersome exchanges. However, the failure to have someone present to translate what is said can seriously impact your clients' ability to communicate effectively with the other party and resolve the conflict.

### 9) Identify Any Cultural Issues

Your awareness (or your clients' awareness) of any cultural differences between the parties or between both parties and the general population may prove useful in bringing about a solution to a conflict.

It is important to discuss with your clients the impact of the conflict with respect to their community. If the parties are both part of a particular cultural community and the conflict becomes known among their friends, business associates, or others in their community, some face-saving device may be needed in order to reach a settlement.

Consider various means of dealing with such an issue, which can be proposed at the appropriate time. For example, one option could be an announcement in a community newsletter or newspaper, indicating that the parties have agreed to participate in a mediation or in settlement discussions to resolve their conflict.

In other cases, if your clients and the other party are from different cultures, they may have had different expectations in dealing with each other. In this situation, it is useful to know about the existing differences. With this knowledge, you can help your clients reach a settlement by explaining the nature of the differences and how they led to the conflict.

## 10) Discuss the Strengths and Weaknesses of the Case

Virtually no case has a 100 percent chance of success before the courts. There are two (or more) parties to a conflict, and each has a different perspective. You should not only review the strengths of your clients' case with them, both with respect to the facts and the law, but also review the weaknesses that will appear in a trial. The strengths can be used as a negotiating tool, but your clients should be aware that their case is not ironclad and that there are reasons to make concessions in order to settle.

In cases where the interpretation of a contract is in issue, if the other party's position is as valid as that of your clients, and if your clients are the plaintiffs, it is unlikely that they will obtain a favourable judgment. When the facts of the case are contested, there is no certainty that your clients' version will prevail. The same is true when the caselaw is divided on the issue in dispute.

Prescription may be an issue. The lack of corroborating evidence with respect to certain facts can be problematic. Your expert's report may not stand up to scrutiny when faced with a contradictory expert report. The caselaw may not support your position. The nature of the case, such as an award of damages, may allow for a certain amount of discretion on the part of a judge. These and many other issues can lead to uncertainty in an outcome when pursuing a lawsuit.

These considerations apply to the other party as well. Your clients should be aware of the strengths of the opposing side. On the other hand, the other party's weaknesses should also be identified, since they can be used to your clients' advantage.

## 11) Identify the Interests and Needs of the Parties

You are aware of the facts and the legal aspects of your clients' case. But what about their emotions? Were they angry about the impact of the other party's words or behaviour? Were they embarrassed, hurt, or humiliated? Were they insulted? Were they distraught, anxious, or fearful?

Your clients' feelings may be as important as the actual facts of the case. As a result, you must find out what emotions your clients have suffered or are suffering and ensure that their feelings are expressed during the mediation session.

Your clients are the ones who must express their feelings when they finish the presentation of their version of the facts. It helps to put some perspective on how your clients reacted to the situation that transpired or how they responded to the conflict. It may also provide a context for some of the demands made in their legal proceedings or the proposals that are made during the negotiations.

There may be other times during the mediation to raise the subject of your clients' feelings once again. This will depend on their interests and needs.

As already indicated in Chapter 3, a person's reputation is an important value for most people. If people claim they have been defamed, they will have a strong interest in clearing a tarnished reputation. Accomplishing this may be more important than financial compensation.

Although it is the role of the mediator to determine the parties' interests and needs, it is also useful for you to do the same. Before attending the mediation, identify what your clients want or need. What are their priorities? Is it recognition that they are seeking? Would an apology be appreciated? Do they need help in dealing with the material damage suffered?

These and other questions of a similar nature will assist you in looking for the kind of solutions that will be important for your clients. If a certain outcome will satisfy their interests and if the other party is willing to meet that interest or need, it can go a long way toward finding a means of coming to a positive resolution of the dispute.

You should also try to determine what would be an essential element for the opposite party. Admittedly, it is difficult to determine before the mediation what their interests could be. It is important to listen to their presentation to learn of any potential interests and needs they may have.

It is also essential to brainstorm with your clients and try to imagine what might motivate the other party to settle. It may simply be a question of money, but frequently, other interests are involved. These interests will be instrumental in bringing about a solution to the conflict.

### 12) Prepare the Documents and Facts Needed

Given that the mediation is not a trial, you will not need to prepare your file in the same way as you do when you go to court. Mediators often will even request that you put away your file.

However, to ensure that you will be fully ready for any eventuality, the following, while non-exhaustive, is a suggested list of documents to have in your possession:

- All the proceedings that have been filed in the case.
- All the documents related to your case (the contract, correspondence, reports, photographs, records, and so on) or, if the litigation has already begun, the exhibits filed by both parties.
- A list of facts in your clients' case in chronological order.
- A list of the means that would be used to establish the veracity of your clients' version of the facts to show the strength of the case if it goes to trial.

It is also advised that you:

- Review the law and its application to your client's case.
- Review the caselaw with respect to both cases that support your client's case and those that do not.

### 13) Prepare a Brief

Some mediators ask for a mediation brief prior to the mediation. This brief should contain a summary of the facts of the case, the legal issues involved, and the position of each of the parties. The necessity for such a brief, in cases involving an evaluative mediator, stems from the fact that such mediators offer an opinion about what the outcome of the case will be if it goes to trial. The mediator's opinion will affect their proposal for a settlement.

However, even in the classic approach to mediation, such a brief or statement is a useful starting point. It provides mediators with an initial understanding of the type of case they will be dealing with, the parties implicated in the dispute, the facts alleged, the legal issues that will be involved if the case proceeds to trial, and the amount of compensation indicated in the court proceedings. The information serves as a basis for mediators to prepare a strategy for the mediation.

Whether the brief is prepared for an evaluative mediator or a classic one, set out your strong arguments clearly and include any supportive documentation you may have as well as audios, videos, and excerpts from examinations or discoveries to enhance your case. Write the brief in a way that is to the point and is presented in straightforward and intelligible language.[4]

The preparation is also useful for you and your clients. It narrows the issues to be discussed and focuses your attention on what your clients will attempt to establish in terms of the facts, their position, and the outcome, whether monetary or non-monetary, that they are seeking.

### 14) Prepare Your Clients to Present the Facts

Usually it is your clients, not you, who will be presenting the facts of the case, their perspective, and what they are seeking. Make sure your clients understand this and do not expect you to present it for them. Since your clients are those who will be telling *their story*, ensure that they are conversant with the facts and issues of their case. They should be prepared to present their version as to what took place between them and the opposing party, without you needing to prompt them during their presentation.

---

4 Stuart Rudner, "Top 12 Tips to Win at Mediation" Rudner Law (19 October 2022), online: www.rudnerlaw.ca/top-12-tips-win-mediation.

It is unlikely that your clients will be allowed to simply read from a pre-written text when describing their version of events. Rather, they will be expected to remember the events and describe them in their own words. They will be allowed notes, however, so it can be useful to list the events that took place, in chronological order, with dates. They will serve as an aid or a reminder for them of the subjects they should discuss and the order in which to talk about them.

As for the issues, your clients will not be expected to discuss the applicable law or the legal principles involved. They will nevertheless have a chance and should be prepared to indicate in laypeople's terms what the issues are for them and how they would like to resolve them. For example, in a case of latent defects in a home, your clients do not have to use such terminology as a latent versus apparent defect. However, they can describe the structural problems they faced shortly after taking possession of the home they purchased from the vendor and explain that there was nothing visible when they visited the property to lead them to foresee the occurrence of the issues they encountered once they began living there.

The list of events or subjects to discuss, together with the dates on which they occurred, will help your clients present the facts of the case and the problems they faced in a chronological order. The list should also include proposals for a settlement.

## 15) Prepare Your Clients to Express Emotions

In a lawsuit, with few exceptions, it is unlikely that you will describe the emotional problems your clients suffered because of the other party's behaviour. The same applies to a trial. It is rare that your clients will have the possibility of testifying as to their emotional state if the case goes to trial. However, in a mediation your clients will have a venue where they will be fully able to express their feelings.

There will be several occasions during the mediation when they can relate how they felt with respect to a particular event or behaviour or how they felt at a particular time in the conflict.

However, the most opportune time to tell the other party about the impact the conflict had on them is immediately after your clients relate their version of the facts. Therefore, your checklist for your clients should include the heading of "emotions" or "feelings" and then an enumeration of the feelings they will relate.

## 16) Carry Out a Mock Presentation

Although a mediation is not as formal as a trial, clients may nevertheless be stressed about attending such a session. To reduce their stress level, it is a good idea to prepare them by carrying out a mock presentation before the mediation. This will not only make your clients feel more comfortable about the upcoming session, but also enable you to make sure they will be able to set out what happened in a coherent manner. It will also provide you with an opportunity to see whether they can express their emotions, which will help humanize the conflict.

Assure your clients that they do not have to memorize their presentation. In fact, it is better that they do not attempt to do so. Having a checklist will be sufficient to help them recall the facts and dates they wish to present in chronological order. It may be necessary for your clients to present their story and their emotions to you more than one time so that they are comfortable and able to express themselves easily at the mediation session. A mock presentation will definitely enhance your clients' comfort with the process.

## 17) Discuss What Your Clients Are Willing to Offer or Accept

If your clients are the plaintiffs, you will have indicated in the lawsuit you prepared on their behalf how much compensation they are seeking. If they are the recipient of a lawsuit, in all probability, you have indicated in their defence that the claim is unfounded.

Before attending court, both parties have a clear idea of their position with respect to the conflict and with respect to the amount of compensation involved. However, frequently they have not considered what is acceptable if they participate in a mediation session.

To ensure that the discussions begin in a fruitful manner and progress well, it is useful to discuss potential proposals with your clients before going to the mediation. It is important for them to accept that they are not there to win the case but rather to reach an outcome that is sufficiently satisfactory, such that they can put the conflict behind them. They should therefore consider and decide what it will take to reach this outcome. The monetary amount may be different from the amount stated in the lawsuit, particularly if the possible outcome of the lawsuit, the costs involved in going to court, and other possible options for settling the case are taken into account.

### 18) Think Outside the Box and Consider Non-monetary Options

Typically, one party seeks monetary compensation from the opposite party. The mediation then is centred on how much the opposing party is ready to pay and whether the final amount offered is acceptable to the party seeking reparation.

However, there may be other ways of finding a solution. It is useful to think outside the box when it comes to floating ideas and suggesting alternatives. It is important to explore with your clients what non-monetary proposals can be raised. Sometimes the alternative proposal may allow the parties to settle.

One example is a case previously mentioned where flooring installed throughout a home had warped shortly after it was put down. Although the lawsuit concluded with a demand for compensation equivalent to the amount the plaintiffs had spent on the new floors, an alternate solution discussed in mediation was having the manufacturer supply another type of wood and having the work redone with this different wood. The plaintiffs, who really wanted new flooring rather than money, were satisfied with this offer and no money was exchanged.

Sometimes, the outcome can come about by a combination of money and an exchange of services.

An example is a case where the defendant was willing to pay the amount plaintiff wanted but did not have the means to do so. The defendant agreed to pay part of the money sought and undertook to provide hairdressing services to the plaintiff to make up the remainder. The parties negotiated the number of visits, the period involved, and the services that would be covered. They reached a conclusion that the plaintiff found acceptable, and the litigation was resolved in this manner.

If your clients are the plaintiffs, you should discuss whether there are any goods, services, or assistance that they would like to have which would bring the case to a close for them. If your clients are the defendants, you should discuss whether there are any goods, services, or assistance that they could provide that may be of interest to the plaintiffs. Since possibilities other than money exist to bring about a settlement, they should be explored with your clients before attending the mediation session.

A useful exercise for your clients is to make a list of possible proposals that are alternatives to money in order to find a means of meeting the parties' interests. This consideration should be applied in all cases, and not only in those cases where the defendants have financial constraints. Both parties can potentially benefit from offering or claiming a non-monetary option as the means of settling or as part of a settlement.

In dealing with solutions that do not involve the payment of money, think about the nature of the claim as well as the nature of the defendant. For example, in a claim against an insurance company, a settlement could include a modification of the insurance policy to cover additional cases of damage.

In a lawsuit involving a manufacturer, a defective product could be replaced with a functional one, with a longer warranty, or with another model of a superior quality.

A lawsuit involving a physical injury sustained by a customer who slipped and fell because of food lying on a grocery store's floor could be settled by the store providing a supply of food to the victim, for a certain period, in addition to monetary compensation.

In a case of a breach of a service contract, as for example by a cleaning operation, the company could offer to render the services or offer additional services in the future, without increasing the cost.

Various possibilities exist for other conflicts. It is important to think about potential means to resolve the issues that can be beneficial for both parties. The possibilities of non-monetary options are numerous. Other examples are set out in Chapter 5, Section E(17).

### 19) Discuss Strategy with Your Clients

It is important to discuss strategy with your clients. This will include such aspects as:

- any "non-starters,"
- the order of the issues to be discussed,
- the use of caucuses,
- the pace of the offers, and
- when to announce your client's bottom line.

These subjects will be discussed again, in Chapter 5, when dealing with your role in the mediation. It is nevertheless advisable to discuss these topics with your clients beforehand, so that your clients have a chance to think about them and are not caught off guard when these issues arise during the mediation.

#### a) Non-starters

Some issues prevent the entire mediation process from taking place, while others are simply more difficult to resolve and should be left for the end of the process. The former relates to an outcome that is essential for one of the parties in order to accept a settlement, but which is so unacceptable to the other party that they would prefer to go to trial.

An example of a non-starter would be a demand for reinstatement in a dismissal case, if reinstatement is an essential condition for the employee in order to settle, while the ex-employer would not consider this scenario under any circumstances. In such cases, clearly the mediation will not work out.

If you suspect that a condition for settlement will evoke a contrary and totally inflexible position on the part of the opposite party, it is advisable to inform the mediator of your client's position and allow the mediator to verify whether your suspicions about the other party are accurate. In the above example, after it is determined that the ex-employer will never consider reinstatement, the preferred approach will be to bring the conflict to another forum, such as a labour tribunal that has jurisdiction to order a reinstatement.

Not all cases involving very contentious issues are problematic. Many can be resolved with compromise. They do not constitute non-starters for the mediation process itself; rather, they are issues that should be put on the back burner and dealt with later in the process, after progress in resolving other issues in the conflict has already taken place.

### b) The Order of Issues to Be Discussed

When the lawsuit includes claims for several items, the mediator may propose the order of the issues to be discussed, or the order may arise from the initial discussions. Although the mediator controls the process, you may nevertheless suggest what subject or subjects you would like to begin with.

Starting with a subject that will readily receive consent from the opposite party will bring positive energy to the process and provide an incentive for the parties to continue to find compromising solutions. Accordingly, discuss whether there is an issue that your clients are willing to forego, or a subject of lesser importance to them such that they are willing to make a concession or accept a compromise. Suggest that your clients propose that subject to the mediator and to the opposing party as a starting point to provide momentum to the negotiations.

As already indicated, the parties should deal with the most difficult subject at the very end of the negotiations. To do otherwise may mean that no common ground is found at the very beginning of the negotiations and the mediation will fail to proceed any further.

It is far easier to conclude an agreement when there is only one issue remaining to be discussed. If all the other issues have already been resolved, the parties understand that coming to an agreement on the final issue means that the entire conflict is settled.

### c) The Use of Caucuses

A caucus is a private meeting that takes place between the mediator, you, and your clients during the mediation process. Everything that is said remains confidential, unless you authorize the mediator to divulge the information to the other party.

The caucus is an essential aspect of the process. It allows each of the parties to meet separately with the mediator and gives them the opportunity to freely discuss their concerns, as well as any issue they consider pertinent, without the fear of compromising their position vis a vis the other party.

The caucus also allows parties to obtain clarification on an issue raised, determine whether or not their position or the other party's position is realistic, re-evaluate an existing offer or negotiation strategy, raise alternatives, obtain new information that may lead to new alternatives, confidentially confide in the mediator, and openly express emotions.

Typically, mediators ask for a caucus. If they do so, they will meet with both parties, one party at a time. Meeting with both parties separately is necessary to maintain the mediators' neutrality and avoid any perception of bias. Mediators may conduct one or several caucuses, meeting the parties as often as is considered to be necessary.

You can also request a caucus with the mediator. If needed, you can also request that you and your clients meet on your own, without the mediator. Mediators will rarely refuse such a request.

It is difficult, if not impossible, to determine before the mediation the timing of a caucus or how many there will be. However, what is important in preparing for the mediation is that both you and your clients are aware of the existence of the caucus and its usefulness.

Your clients should be aware that they can ask you to request a caucus when they wish to discuss a proposal that is presented to them, a proposal they wish to make, their concerns, or any other aspect of the case in private with you and the mediator. During the mediation session, you can use the caucus as a strategic means of dealing with an impasse in the negotiations and of determining how you will continue to proceed.

### d) The Pace of the Proposals

The mediation process can move at a quick pace or a slow pace. It most often depends on the parties. It also depends on whether or not there are many issues in dispute. Obviously, more time is required when several issues must be resolved. The pace of the negotiations may also depend on whether only monetary compensation is involved or whether other avenues are also considered.

Frequently, the parties do not want to show how much they are willing to offer or concede and they move very gradually from their initial position. Impasses arise. Neither party is prepared to yield. Caucuses take place. More offers are made. The parties slowly move toward a more middle ground in their attempt to find a mutually acceptable solution.

When both parties have already decided on their bottom line, they may move relatively quickly to divulge their positions, and determine the outcome of the conflict, with very little negotiating. Such an approach may involve one or two offers followed by a caucus where one of the parties advises the mediator that they are prepared to offer a certain amount of money and it is a final offer; if it is not accepted, they will go to trial.

The opposite party, when hearing this position, only has the possibility of accepting or rejecting the offer, not of negotiating alternatives. In such a case, the session will end quickly, one way or the other.

Before attending the mediation, you should discuss the question of the pace of the negotiations with your clients. Have they had any experience negotiating before? What is their style? Are they comfortable moving quickly or would they prefer to move at a gradual pace?

These are some of the areas that you should explore with your clients. You should also advise them that there is always the possibility to deal with the situation differently at the mediation session. There, you will see whether or not the other party is prepared to make significant counter proposals to your propositions. In this way, you will be able to evaluate the other party's momentum and, if necessary, adjust your pace accordingly.

### 20) Determine Your Clients' Bottom Line

It may be beneficial to establish your clients' bottom line—that is, your clients' final position which will not change. What is the point at which they would be prepared to go to trial, rather than accept the opposite party's final proposition?

If your clients are the complainants or the plaintiffs, you cannot determine beforehand how much the defendants will be willing to pay or whether a satisfactory alternative solution will be proposed. However, you can determine before the mediation what minimum amount of money will induce your clients to settle and whether any other conditions or alternatives exist that will bring about this result.

The same applies to the recipients of the complaint or the defendants. While you cannot determine before the mediation what compromise the complainants or plaintiffs will make at the mediation, you can determine with your clients what the maximum amount of money they will be willing to offer and whether there are any other conditions or alternatives they can propose to sweeten the deal.

At the same time, it is important to advise your clients not to take a rigid stand. The bottom line they considered should not be etched in stone. Although having a bottom line ensures that your clients will not be pushed to concede too much because of pressure from the opposite party, adopting a bottom line prevents your clients from thinking outside the box and finding another solution that could be beneficial for both parties. Often, the bottom line chosen by clients who are the plaintiffs is too high. Conversely, if your clients are the defendants, their bottom line may be too low.

In addition, once adopted, it may be difficult for your clients to change their position without losing face. Moreover, during the mediation session itself, new facts may emerge, and proposals may be presented that were unforeseen before the mediation, such that it will become clear that the pre-established bottom line should not be absolute.

Notwithstanding the determination of a bottom line, you may wish to point out that although your clients or the other party may declare that their offer or position is final, that may not always be the case. There may be some small movement by either party, even toward the end of the mediation, in order to reach a deal.

## 21) Discuss Your Clients' BATNA and Best- and Worst-Case Scenarios

Parties negotiate to get a better outcome to their conflict than if they go to trial. However, any potential agreement they are considering should be compared with the alternative that they will obtain if they go to court. This is called your Best Alternative to a Negotiated Agreement (BATNA).

It is useful before attending the mediation to have a good idea of what the best-case scenario and the worst-case scenario are if your clients do not settle. In other words, if they fail to reach an agreement and go to trial, what is the likely outcome of their case?

Your clients can make a claim for a certain amount of money. Even though you indicated to your clients that they have a particularly good case, and you expect them to win following a trial, you cannot be certain of the outcome. There is always a risk in going to court. The outcome may be totally unexpected.

As you are aware, a judgment can range from totally granting a claim to completely rejecting it. Even in cases where your clients obtain a judgment in their favour, they may be awarded considerably less than they anticipate. If they are in defence, they may find that they are ordered to pay much more than they expected. In either case, there is a likelihood that one of the parties or both will not be satisfied.

The better your clients' BATNA or alternative is, the more leverage your clients will have in negotiating the terms of an agreement. Accordingly, a realistic evaluation of the potential outcome of your clients' case, if they go to court, will help your clients determine how much or what conditions are minimally acceptable to them and whether or not to settle.

### 22) Discuss the Costs of Not Settling

In the same way that your clients should have a realistic evaluation of their strengths and weaknesses as well as the potential outcome if they go to trial, they should also be aware of the estimated costs involved.

The judgment will provide the amount, if any, payable to the plaintiffs. However, in addition to the judgment, in determining the outcome of a lawsuit there are court fees and bailiff costs, as well as your legal fees and expenses and in certain cases, expert fees as well.

When discussing the best- and worst-case scenarios, these fees and costs should be factored in and written down so that your clients have a more realistic evaluation of the financial situation they potentially face at the end of the process. After considering the total cost of going to court, which includes the emotional cost, the stress, the uncertainty, the time involved, and the impact on your clients' business or work, your clients may be more disposed to settle.

In addition, your clients should be reminded that in the mediation process, they have a measure of control over the outcome.

If the parties do not settle, they will no longer have any control over the resolution of the case. A judge will render a decision based on the law and the facts of the case, without taking into consideration the parties' emotions or their interests and needs.

*chapter five*

# The Mediation Process

Lawyers often think that they can wait until the mediation session to figure out how they will negotiate a settlement or help their clients to do so. This is not effective. While it is not possible to determine beforehand how the opposing party will act or what proposals will be put on the table, there are nevertheless many aspects of the negotiations that can be controlled and many aspects that lawyers can prepare for.

As an example, it is possible to defuse an angry reaction by expressing understanding of the other party's position and by using the technique of reformulating. In my mediation sessions, lawyers who were adept at negotiating not only used such methods but also helped their clients by noting who was making decisions on the opposite side. Similarly, the lawyers who were skilled in negotiating could help clients who were very slow and cautious deal with the pace of the negotiations by encouraging them in the privacy of a caucus to compromise less in order to keep pace with the proposals of the other party. In addition to using the caucus in a beneficial manner, lawyers familiar with the process were able to deal with impasses effectively or, at the very least, were able to help during the mediation to overcome a blockage when it took place.

Most importantly, lawyers who are grounded in the concept of classic mediation are aware of the importance of the parties' interests. They are able to steer their negotiations toward the interests and needs of the parties such that they do not get bogged down in their respective positions.

This chapter outlines the various challenges that lawyers face in the mediation process and the techniques that are available to lawyers to be able to help their clients negotiate effectively, evaluate the options on the table, and confidently accept or refuse the final settlement proposal(s).

## A. AN OVERVIEW OF THE MEDIATION PROCESS

Your clients may have never participated in a mediation session, and for them to be comfortable with the process, it is important that they have a good idea of how it will proceed. While mediators vary in terms of their style and approach, most experienced mediators use a common practice that involves a step-by-step method.

The following is an overview of the process, which will be explained in more detail subsequently.

### 1) Introduction

Mediators will begin with introductions, and, amongst other topics, will proceed to discuss the goal of mediation, the role of the participants, and how the mediation process will take place.

### 2) The Parties' Presentation of Their Version of the Facts

The parties have the opportunity of relating the events leading to their dispute, and both you and your clients will have the possibility of learning about the other party's perspective, interests, needs, and concerns.

### 3) The Interests and Needs of the Parties

The parties, during the presentation of the facts, express their feelings and emotions. The parties will be able to hear the perspective of the other party, as well as the impact the conflict has had on them and what will motivate them to settle. In this step, the interests and needs of the parties are identified, with a view of finding solutions that will meet these interests and needs.

### 4) The Negotiation and Selection of Options

At this stage, the parties will make proposals and counter proposals in negotiating options for a mutually beneficial settlement. The discussions may take place in a plenary session, with everyone present, or in caucuses. During the negotiations, you will help your clients and the mediator to brainstorm, identify criteria for a settlement that is fair to both parties, attempt to overcome impasses when they occur, and achieve a consensus with respect to a possible solution.

As counsel, you will play an active role during this part of the process. You will:

- assist your clients in the presentation of proposals,
- evaluate proposals made,
- brainstorm with your clients,
- encourage them to think outside the box,
- determine when a caucus should take place and request caucuses, as needed,
- obtain further information,
- encourage your clients to reconsider,
- suggest compromises to be made,
- recommend proposals to meet common interests,
- assist your clients in determining their final bottom line,
- provide strategic and legal advice throughout the process, and
- protect your clients' interests.

### 5) The Closing

If the parties settle their conflict, the lawyers will draft the agreement, taking into consideration that it must be clear and contain all the pertinent elements.

The parties may reach a partial settlement, or they may not come to any agreement, which will ultimately result in going to court.

## B. OPENING BY THE MEDIATOR

The mediation session begins with the opening by the mediator.[1] Although you have described the process for your clients, it is always useful for them to hear the mediator explain the process to the participants. Neither you nor your clients have any active role to play at this initial stage.

### 1) Seating Arrangements

Some mediators prefer to seat the parties, while others allow the parties to place themselves around the table. If the mediator has not placed the parties around the conference table, it is preferable, if possible, to seat your clients facing the opposing party. It is also preferable for your clients to sit closer to the mediator than you, since in most mediations your clients will be presenting their story and will be dealing directly with the mediator and the other party.

### 2) Introductions

Typically, the mediator will begin by with the introductions, asking the parties and their lawyers to introduce themselves to each other. Then some mediators will congratulate the parties for choosing mediation and will express their confidence that the parties will succeed in resolving their conflict and come to an agreement.

1 There are no set rules for the mediator's comments to the parties at the beginning of the mediation session. The information contained in this section is based on the way the author generally proceeds, and it corresponds with basic training for mediators.

### 3) Verifications

The mediator will verify whether the parties are present and available for the duration of the process, and whether each party has the authority to settle. If this is not the case, the mediator will want assurance that the person with the authority to settle can be reached throughout the process and will be able to follow the offers and counteroffers. If other participants are present, the mediator will determine what their role will be.

### 4) The Goal of the Mediation

Parties sometimes come to a mediation session erroneously believing that a decision will be rendered in their case and that the mediator will determine liability. However, the parties will be reminded that the objective of the session is to find a means of resolving the conflict that is satisfactory for both parties; it is not to determine who is right. The mediator will explain that the mediation is called a *win-win process* and that neither party should expect that they will achieve the outcome set out in their legal proceedings. Both parties will need to compromise and work together collaboratively to find a solution to their conflict.

### 5) Advantages of the Mediation Process

The mediator will list the many advantages of mediation, emphasizing the most important one being the possibility for the parties to determine the content of their agreement, such that it resolves all the issues between them and can even include aspects that a judge cannot order.

### 6) The Role of the Participants

Mediators will refer to the role of each of the participants. They will begin by explaining their role to the parties, namely that they are neutral and impartial and (where the mediator does not have an evaluative function) will not render a decision or decide the outcome of the mediation; rather, the mediator's role is to help the parties to communicate more effectively with each other and reach a mutually satisfactory solution.

Mediators will then advise the parties that they will be taking centre stage. They are the ones who will present their versions of the facts of the case, and they will have sufficient time to do so. They are also the ones who will discuss various options for a settlement and try to find a solution that is acceptable to both.

As for the lawyers, mediators will remind them that their role is not to try to litigate the case or raise legal issues but to collaborate and help the parties reach an agreement.

### 7) How the Mediation Will Proceed

Mediators will outline how the mediation will take place, explaining the steps that will be followed. They will also explain the plenary meetings where everyone is present and the caucuses where they will meet with each party and their lawyer privately. They will tell the parties that, in a caucus, the parties will be able to provide them with information or discuss any matter that they may not be willing to share with the other party. They will explain that everything that is said during a caucus is confidential, unless the party provides authorization to divulge what was said to the other party.

### 8) The Rules

While there are no formal rules, mediators request that each party listen when the other party is speaking and not interrupt the presentation. In addition, it is expected that the parties will act in a civil manner and be respectful with one another. Mediators inform the parties that insulting or abusive language, as well as threats or any intimidating behaviour, are not acceptable in the mediation.

### 9) Confidentiality of the Process

Mediators advise the parties that the process itself is not recorded and is confidential. They explain the advantage of the confidential nature of the process, namely that it allows the parties to be open without the fear that what they express during the mediation can be used against them, if the case goes to trial. The importance of not divulging anything that was said or written during the mediation is emphasized. Some mediators will advise both the lawyers and the parties that if they take any notes, they must be destroyed at the end of the mediation session. This is the time the confidentiality agreement is usually presented to the participants for signature.

### 10) The Outcome of the Mediation

If the parties reach an agreement, mediators will tell them that the lawyers will draft the agreement and they will subsequently desist from their lawsuit. If the parties do not settle, there is no impact on their lawsuit. Their case continues to proceed through the judicial system as though they had not participated in a mediation. In addition, the mediation will not influence the court proceedings, since whatever was said at the mediation session cannot be divulged in a trial. Moreover, because the mediation file is kept separately from the court file, the judge presiding over the trial will not even be aware that the parties attempted to resolve their conflict by means of mediation.

### 11) Commitment to the Process

Following this opening presentation, mediators will ask the parties if they understand the process and if they have any questions. Mediators refer to the informal and voluntary aspect of mediation and seek assurance that the parties are committed to trying to resolve their conflict amicably. After any questions are answered, the mediation moves to the next step.

### 12) The Duration of the Introduction

In cases where the parties have an ongoing personal or work-related relationship and have experience with the mediation process, such as in the context of labour relations, a lengthy introduction is not required. The mediators' preliminary remarks may be noticeably short.

However, in other instances, and particularly when the parties have never attended a mediation session and are generally rather stressed, a detailed explanation is warranted. This not only ensures that the parties fully understand the process and how it will unfold but also that they have sufficient time to become more relaxed and prepared to actively participate in the session.

## C. PRESENTATION OF THE FACTS

Various terms have been given to describe this step in the process. It may be called *The Parties' Opening Statement* or the *Communication of Events* or the *Presentation of the Facts*. It refers to the presentation by each party of their version of the facts and includes their perspective of the conflict.

Most mediators prefer that the parties, rather than the lawyers, explain what transpired, since the aim is for them to communicate with each other and try to end their conflict. However, there are certain mediators who will permit the lawyers to present the summary of the facts on behalf of their clients. Consequently, the lawyer's role in the presentation is explained first in the next section, followed by the more common situation, where the clients present their versions of the facts.

As indicated in the Introduction, some lawyers come to a mediation prepared to begin negotiating immediately. However, there is a process that must be followed. Knowledge of the background of a case and the other party's perceptions of what transpired are necessary in order to understand how the opposing party will consider an offer. In addition, the parties may not be ready to engage in the negotiations if they have not had an opportunity to express their experiences, emotions, and demands. Allow the process to unfold gradually. There are many advantages to hearing the facts presented by the parties. The information gained will help you immensely in the ensuing negotiations.

### 1) The Lawyers' Introductory Presentation

In instances where mediators ask you to present your clients' version of the facts involved,[2] it is important to remember to address your remarks to the opposing party, rather than to the mediator. It is the other party, and in particular the person having the authority to settle, who will ultimately decide whether to accept a final proposal if a settlement is to take place. It is unlikely that you will convince the opposing party, as you would with a judge, that your clients' position is right. However, you may be able to show the opposing party that their case is not ironclad. It is important to remember that even when the parties do not agree on all the facts of the case, or on whose position is correct in law, a settlement can still be achieved.

Be prepared, with supporting evidence, to support your clients' claim. In your presentation, lay out the facts in clear, chronological order. Use layperson's terms and not legal jargon, which may be incomprehensible to the other party. Be concise and try not to drown the essential facts with many unimportant details. Show the opposing party that you are prepared, that you have objective evidence, and that your clients' case is credible.

Talk about the risks of going to trial. Raise doubts about the adversary's chance of winning in court. Speak about the necessity

---

2 In most cases, it is the parties who present the facts of the case. This author never asks the lawyers to give an introductory presentation. However, since some mediators ask that the lawyers speak on behalf of their clients, the key points of a lawyer's presentation are provided here, based in part on the article by Joan Stearns Johnsen, "Opening Statements in Mediation" American Bar Association (24 February 2021), online: www.americanbar.org/groups/litigation/committees/alternative-dispute-resolution/practice/2021/opening-statements-in-mediation.

of having an open mind and the need for both parties to compromise in the hope that they will reach an equitable solution to their litigation.

It is important to use neutral, even encouraging, language. Do not use provocative or accusatory language. You will not achieve anything by threatening, raising your voice, or using absolute terms such as *never* or *out of the question*. It is far more helpful to show some empathy for the other party and counsel and indicate your appreciation for their participation in the mediation. Finally, show optimism and end on a positive note by telling the other party that you trust both parties will be reasonable and believe that the mediation will be successful.

### 2) The Presentation by the Parties

In most instances, mediators will ask the parties to relate what took place and what led to their conflict. While some mediators request that each party speak to the mediator, others will ask the parties to address each other instead.

There is no set order for the presentation. However, typically the person who has instituted the action, or who has initiated the complaint, will be asked to begin first, unless the other party prefers to start.

Each party is provided with the opportunity to fully present their version of the facts in the case. The opposite party is told not to intervene until the first party has terminated their presentation. Then the party who has not spoken will have the opportunity to present their version of the facts.

Typically, the parties are told that when one of them is talking, the other party must listen and not look through the file, talk to their lawyer, or interrupt. If the parties disagree with anything the opposing party says during the presentation, they should note it. They will subsequently have their turn of uninterrupted time, to refute any of the facts alleged.

The aim is not to convince the mediator that the facts presented are well founded, since the mediator is not determining the outcome of the dispute. As already indicated, it is the role of the parties to determine the outcome of their conflict.

Whether your clients are addressing the mediator or the other party, they have a story to tell. Their presentation will allow the opposing party to hear your clients' version of the facts and possibly some information the other party may not have heard before.

Equally important, your clients' presentation will indicate to the opposing party what impact the opposing party's words or actions had on them.

This step gives your clients the opportunity not only to tell their story but also to express their feelings. Such feelings may include those of humiliation, fear, despair, helplessness, frustration, anger, the desire for revenge, or any other emotion. How your clients relate their story, and emotions, will set the tone of the mediation.

In presenting their story, it is useful for your clients to:

- Address the opposite party (and counsel) and, whenever possible, talk to them directly, rather than to the mediator.
- Begin with how the parties met. Most mediators ask the parties to start with how the conflict began. However, in cases where the parties had an ongoing relationship, it is beneficial for your clients to talk about the positive aspects of their business relationship, professional association, friendship, or other dealings with each other. Beginning in this manner highlights what each appreciated in the other party and can reduce tensions and hostility. As well, beginning in this way can potentially provide the basis for re-establishing what had been a good relationship in the past.
- Set out the facts in chronological order, using a checklist to help recall the specific events and dates.
- Detail the incidents or events that led to the conflict.
- Express their feelings by describing how they felt when a particular statement was made against them, a particular action was taken, or a particular situation occurred that impacted them negatively. It is important for your clients to say: *We felt*

*. . . when you said . . .* or *We perceived . . .* or *We understood that . . . when you . . .* instead of making accusations or claiming that the opposing party was abusive, insulting, or lying.
- Avoid using legal jargon, which the opposing party may not comprehend.
- Be respectful of the other party.
- Avoid insults and abusive language when discussing the statements or actions that led to the lawsuit or conflict. Even when your clients doubt the accuracy of the other party's version of the facts or believe that the other party failed to act in good faith, they should not resort to name calling. While your clients may feel angry and hostile toward the opposite party, insulting that party will only have a negative effect and will usually generate equally aggressive behaviour on the part of the opposing party. Insults are not conducive to a settlement. They may even prompt the opposing party to leave the mediation.
- Express your appreciation that the opposing party agreed to participate in the mediation.

During the presentation, or after your clients have concluded, you may intervene to help your clients fill in any gaps in their story that they forgot to mention or to talk about any aspect of the case that they may have failed to bring up.

Although you cannot assume your usual litigation role of examining your clients or cross-examining the opposite party, you can nevertheless deal with any omissions in your clients' version of the facts. You can also pose questions to clarify ambiguities in the parties' stories. Rather than ask direct questions to elicit your clients' response in instances where they forgot to talk about an aspect of their story, it is preferable to suggest the subject matter to your clients.

For example, in a dismissal case, rather than ask your clients a series of specific questions such as how long they were given to leave the premises, what chance they were given to say goodbye to colleagues, what they were allowed to take with them, whether they left on their own or were escorted out, and so on, you should simply prompt your clients by asking them to describe in detail what took place after they were called into the boss's office and told that they were fired.

There are usually further exchanges between the parties to deal with any issue of disagreement, after each one presents their version of the facts. The parties may have strong, harsh words for each other. Each party may have reason to be angry with the opposing party. It is not unusual for the parties to continue to argue about what, in fact, transpired, and whether the version of the opposite party was correct. On the other hand, the exchange of stories can also result in an acknowledgement of some of the common facts in the conflict.

It is not important for your clients to establish that their version is the true one. A lack of agreement on the facts of the case is not an impediment to concluding an agreement, particularly since the purpose of the mediation is not to determine who is right or who is liable.

Finally, in cases where the parties do not speak the same language and each one tells their story in their own language, make sure that your clients understand what the other party has said. It is useful for them to use a signal to indicate their lack of understanding so that you can intervene and assist them.

### 3) The Importance of the Presentation

It is important for each party to hear the opposite party's version. Frequently, they have never had a chance to discuss what took place and what led to the conflict. They often have not had the possibility of confronting each other about their respective behaviour. Probably, they also have never had the opportunity to express their emotions about what transpired.

This may also be the case for the lawyers. Your clients have already discussed their case with you. However, presumably, as a lawyer, you have focused on the legal aspects, in determining whether you can obtain a favourable judgment, rather than determining the underlying cause of the problem or your clients' feelings.

The facts and the law are essential in successfully litigating a case in court, but other elements come into play when it comes to resolving the conflict, including each party's perceptions, their reaction to the past events, and their ensuing emotions.

In fact, very often both parties come to the mediation with strong feelings. Their emotions take over and become more important than their factual differences. Those strong emotions are often the reason that the parties have not succeeded in resolving their dispute in the past.

Moreover, both parties often insist that their version is the true version, and they will not back down from their positions or reconsider. If the case were to be held before the courts, it would be necessary to determine whose version was accurate. However, in the case of a mediation, this determination is not necessary.

What is important is that both parties have a forum where they can explain their respective perceptions and positions, and where they can vent their feelings. The presentation of the facts gives each party the opportunity to provide whatever explanations are needed, so that the other party can hear and understand them.

As indicated above, this may be the first time the parties have been able to convey information that they have never disclosed to the other party. This may be the first time that one or the other party hears facts they were not aware of. This may also be the first time the parties will be subject to considerations that they had not previously considered.

The parties' presentations are also useful for you as the lawyer. It allows you to have an idea of how your clients present themselves and how their case will be perceived if the parties do not settle and you ultimately go to court.

It also provides you with a portrait of the other party's case, giving you not only a sense of both the strengths and weaknesses of their case, but also an idea of their interests and the needs that must be met for a settlement to take place.

It goes without saying that the presentation is also important for mediators. It allows them to hear each party's story, to learn as much as possible about the differing views of the facts in the case, and to understand the parties' different perceptions. It is also a means for mediators to comprehend what gave rise to the conflict and what the interests and needs of the parties may be.

Lawyers often are anxious to begin negotiating as quickly as possible, since presumably both parties know the facts of the case. However, as already indicated, it is important not to pass over a step in the process. If the parties have not had a chance to tell their version of the story or say everything that they wish to say concerning their case, or if they have not had a chance to express their emotions, they will constantly return to the facts or to their emotions at a later stage, and little progress will be made.

This means that you must ensure that your clients have told their whole narrative and have nothing more to add before the mediator moves on to the next stage of the process.

### 4) Active Listening

It is important to actively listen to the opposite party and pay close attention to what has been said. By listening, you and your clients will hear how that party has perceived the events that gave rise to the conflict. You will learn whether or not they have been emotionally impacted and if so, in what way. If you want the other party to understand and appreciate how your clients feel about what has occurred, then your clients must start by being open to what the opposing party is telling them.

Often, rather than listening to what the opposing party is saying, each party is thinking about a possible response. Whatever either party says will be meaningless unless the other party is listening. If your clients interrupt or argue with the opposite party, they will not hear what was said; they will not be aware of the opposite party's perspective; they will not know what their interests are or how the conflict can be resolved. Your clients may not agree with the opposing party, but it is nevertheless important that they try to understand that party's point of view.

Active listening allows your clients to better understand the other party's position and concerns. If the facts presented by the other party are not clear, your clients should ask for an explanation, as for example: *It is not clear to us what you meant when you said...* or alternatively: *Did we correctly understand that...?* which gives the other party the chance to explain the statements made.

After the other party provides an explanation, it is appropriate for your clients to indicate that they understand what the other party has said, even though you and your clients may not agree. For example, your clients could say: *We understand your concerns, although we do not agree with you.* If the opposing party and counsel understand that your clients are listening to them, it will build trust and enhance the possibility of a settlement.

### 5) Non-verbal Communication

It is important not only to listen carefully to what the other party is saying but also to note the opposing party's non-verbal communication. Non-verbal communication refers to the transmission of information by means of gestures, facial expressions, and body language. More than half of our communication is by means of body language and facial expressions. Various parts of our body provide clues as to what we are thinking. Consider the movement of our eyes, the movement of our hands, the placement of our arms, our posture, and so on.[3] Non-verbal communication can affect how the parties relate to each other.

While spoken language conveys a message, body language and other non-verbal cues are often more important in communication. Is the other party whispering to their lawyer? Are they focused on the documents on file? Is the other party looking at a smart phone, responding to emails or text messages? These are all indications as to whether the other party is listening. If the opposite party and counsel are not paying attention to what your clients are saying, bring your concerns to their attention or raise this fact with the mediator. You may remind the other party that

---

3 Laura López Viera, "The influence of Nonverbal Language on Mediation" (2015) 8:2 *Revista de Mediación* e6.

your clients listened carefully to what they had to say and that you expect them to do likewise.

You should also note other signs of non-verbal communication.[4] For example, does the other party appear relaxed or tense? Does the other party seem to be confident, or seek the attorney's approval when speaking? Does the other party make eye contact or avoid it? Are their arms crossed? Are they nodding or shaking their head while your clients are talking? Are they rolling their eyes? Are they frowning?

These signs are important in understanding the other party's attitude, emotions, and feelings.[5] For example, nodding the head usually means agreement with what was said and encourages the speaker to continue, while shaking the head indicates complete disagreement with what the speaker is saying. A yawn can be an indication of tiredness, but it could also convey boredom on the part of the listener. Looking away from the speaker may also be a sign of disinterest. Tapping fingers on the tabletop is indicative of impatience. A smile is a considered to be a display of happiness but slamming a fist on the table will indicate anger. The speaker who points a finger at the opposite party may be trying to emphasize a point, but this gesture could also be considered threatening. Crossed arms usually indicate a lack of openness while rolling the eyes can mean that the listener thinks what the speaker is saying is preposterous. Avoidance of eye contact could signal insecurity. Other non-verbal clues include body posture. For example, pulling the chair closer to the table and leaning in might illustrate an interest in what the speaker is saying, while leaning back or moving away from the table could show a lack of interest in the communication.

It is important to observe and note all the non-verbal language used by the parties. It can provide important clues in evaluating

4 Joan Kessler, "The Significance of Nonverbal Communication in Mediation and Arbitration" (13 August 2021), online: https://mediate.com/the-significance-of-nonverbal-communication-in-mediation-and-arbitration.

5 Ronald S. Tolentino, "The Use of Non-Verbal Communication in Mediation" 2nd AMA Conference (24 February 2011), online: http://barcouncil.org.my/conference1/pdf/3.NONVERBALCOMMUNICATIONANDMEDIATION.pdf.

the opposing party's reactions, emotions, and position with respect to a prestation or a proposal.

However, it is also important to remember that these body language cues are not reliable across the board. Different cultures have different body language customs, while neurodivergent people often display body language and facial responses that are different from those common among neurotypical people. For example, many autistic people struggle to maintain eye contact, so in that case a lack of eye contact would not signal insincerity. Take body language and non-verbal clues into consideration but avoid making negative assumptions about the parties based solely on these observations.

## D. EXPRESSING THE INTERESTS AND NEEDS OF THE PARTIES

As indicated in a previous section, if you are preparing a lawsuit, you will consider the facts in the legal context and determine the nature of the conflict; this could include, for example, latent defects, breach of contract, medical malpractice, insurance claims, unpaid fees, constructive dismissal, divorce proceedings, copyright infringement, and so on.

If you represent the plaintiffs, you will establish the amount of compensation you believe is payable in the case. If you represent the defendants, you will deny any responsibility on your clients' behalf and indicate that they refuse to pay any compensation.

Again, as already stated, lawyers rarely try to determine their clients' interests and needs, which is essential in any attempt to attain a settlement.

Unless the mediator's role is to provide a neutral assessment of the outcome of the case in court or in an arbitration, the next step in the mediation process is to establish each party's interests and needs. Mediators will try to determine the interests and needs of both parties. However, it is equally important for you, as a lawyer, to be concerned with the underlying issues of your clients and the other party.

You have learned, in preparing for the mediation, what your clients' interests are. It is equally important to note what the other party has said to learn what factors are important to them and what options can eventually be suggested to satisfy their needs.

In Chapter 3, we provided a list of various interests and needs that parties may have. The interests include that of confidentiality, obtaining an explanation, respect, an apology, or an interest in re-establishing a relationship. This list is not exhaustive. It is important is to keep these and other interests in mind when negotiating and searching for a solution.

The interests and needs of both parties may coincide. In such a case, there is common ground and it is easier for the parties to come to an agreement. An example is a case where one party wants to preserve their reputation and keep the matter private, and the other party also seeks confidentiality at all costs.

Consider the case of a medical malpractice lawsuit where a facelift operation goes badly and results in a crooked smile. The doctor and the hospital, concerned about their reputation and their standing, will clearly want confidentiality. The patient may also want confidentiality, not wishing that others know about the operation. The patient may claim publicly that a dental procedure nicked a nerve, rather than admitting to having undergone a facelift. The commonality is that both are concerned about their reputation and both want to keep the matter private.

Even in cases where the interests and needs do not coincide, a settlement can be achieved if the interests of one party can be satisfied by the other. Such is the case, for example, where one party seeks an apology. If the other party is willing to apologize, or even express any regret about what took place, it can be of tremendous help in bringing the parties together.

An agreement can still be reached even when the interests of both parties are completely different if they each obtain what they need to move on.

Consider the same case concerning the facelift. The patient's monetary claim may be excessively high, and too high for the doctor. However, the crooked mouth can be rectified by another intervention. The patient's interest is in having the crooked mouth repaired, while the doctor's interest is in satisfying the patient and in paying as little compensation as possible. The parties could agree that the operation be redone. Such an agreement could resolve the case if the issue of the crooked mouth is resolved, or it could considerably reduce the amount payable to the patient.

Therefore, during the presentation of the facts of the case, it is useful to keep a list of possible interests with you and note any statement made, or any issue raised by the other party, that could be explored and assist in finding a solution.

For your clients to obtain what they need, they must be specific not only about what they are seeking but also about the legitimacy of their claim.

Consider the case of a job loss. The employee, a senior manager, is seeking significant compensation for having been laid off. The company had undergone a reorganization and combined two positions, selecting another manager to fill the job. The company offered only a nominal amount of severance to the manager, who now no longer has a job. The question to consider is what the basis is for the manager to claim such a large sum of money from the company.

The manager is not only angry about the loss of employment but is also distressed. The manager has a family to feed and a mortgage to pay, and needs funds to cover expenses until another position is found. In order for the opposing side to consider the manager's claim, it is necessary to explain the manager's needs and indicate that the amount requested is fair, under the circumstances. The manager should emphasize the length of time worked for the company and the difficulty in obtaining equivalent employment. Moreover, an objective standard should be provided to the company, such as a precedent in the caselaw for a similar job loss.

Rather than blaming the other party for the situation your clients find themselves in, it is more beneficial for them to talk about what they want for the future.

## E. NEGOTIATION AND SELECTION OF OPTIONS

### 1) To Reach This Step

Before negotiating the options, the mediator has been actively listening, directing the discussions, and ensuring that both parties have had an opportunity to fully express everything they wish to say before moving on to the next step.

Since the focus of this text is not on the role of the mediator, it suffices to indicate that during the presentations, the mediator will ask relevant questions to elicit as much information as possible and will use techniques such as reframing to clarify issues, create different perspectives, neutralize toxic language, identify common problems, and establish common objectives.

The mediator usually presents a summary of each party's presentation, briefly reviewing the salient facts that were presented and the respective positions of both parties, while at the same time showing an understanding of the issues raised as well as empathy for both parties.

While listening and questioning the parties, the mediator is looking for common elements. If they become apparent, the mediator will point to them as a means of showing the participants that there is a particularly good basis for coming to an agreement. Frequently, a flip chart or blackboard will be used to track the common interests and needs of the parties.

### 2) The Approach to Take: Positioned/Competitive Versus Principled/Collaborative Negotiations

Negotiating with another person is natural. You have, in all probability, engaged in it, in your everyday lives. Consider the many times you have discussed with your friends or family where to go for a vacation, where to go for dinner, or which movie to watch. Your first suggestion may be met with a counter proposal. In this case, you may maintain your position or relent somewhat, presenting another proposal. The back and forth of proposals and counter proposals continues until you reach an agreement.

There are different negotiating styles. Some negotiation experts talk about five styles, referred to as competing, avoiding, accommodating, compromising, and collaborating.[6] However, most negotiators refer to the two main types of negotiating, namely competitive or positional negotiations and collaborative or principled negotiations.

Competitive or positional negotiations consist of bargaining based on an adopted position. These type of negotiators are known as a hard bargainers. Their goal is to win. They will dig into their positions, demand concessions, and apply pressure to achieve the result they want. The gain achieved by one party will be at the expense of the other. This method is often used when the matter in dispute is not negotiable or when the object is to obtain results very quickly—as, for example, in the sale of an object to a stranger.

At the other extreme, some negotiators, called soft bargainers, are prepared to accommodate, particularly when a relationship is involved. Their goal is to reach an agreement. They will avoid confrontation and make concessions in the hope of maintaining a relationship or a friendship. Parties may reach an agreement more quickly when both have the same negotiating style than when two people with different styles negotiate. In competitive or positional bargaining, the negotiations are often a contest of wills, and the outcome will generally be more favourable to the hard bargainer than to the soft bargainer.

When the hard bargainer does not dominate the soft player and the gains are not all one-sided, this type of bargaining often leads to a mechanical splitting of the differences between the parties' final positions, in a monetary dispute. Alternatively, when neither one is willing to compromise, an impasse will occur, and there will be no possibility of a settlement. This approach is not very efficient, and once the process is over, there is little possibility of re-establishing or continuing a relationship.

---

6 Calum Coburn, "Negotiating Conflict Styles," online: https://hms.harvard.edu/sites/default/files/Departments/Ombuds%20Office/files/NegotiationStyles.Understanding%20the%20Five%20Negotiation%20Styles.by%20Calum%20Coburn_0.pdf.

The authors Roger Fisher and William Ury in their well-known book, *Getting to Yes: Negotiating Agreement Without Giving In,*[7] suggest an alternative way of negotiating, where the approach is neither hard bargaining nor soft bargaining.

The method is called *principled negotiations* or *collaborative negotiations*. This approach is an alternative to that of competitive or positional bargaining, revolving around each party's position. The focus of collaborative negotiations is on the parties' respective interests. This method is considered to be a *win-win* approach, with the objective of meeting the interests and needs of both parties. It is most useful when relationships are involved, as well as in situations where the goal is to find a solution that is acceptable to both parties.

Collaborative negotiation is the method that is generally used in mediation sessions. The negotiations are aimed at meeting the interests of the parties, proposing options, evaluating the options, and reaching a mutually satisfying agreement, using fair and objective criteria. People must work together to resolve their problem, as opposed to being combative and attacking each other. The aim is to increase the pie, rather than divide it.

Consider the following as an example of negotiating by questioning the reasoning of the other party and insisting on the use of objective criteria.[8]

A woman, contacting an insurance company, reports the theft of a car. It was a three-year-old Mercedes-Benz, well maintained, in excellent condition, with low mileage. The price initially paid for the vehicle was $120,000.

The woman's insurance agent offers $50,000 for the vehicle. The woman objects, saying that it is not possible to buy another Mercedes or even another luxury car with that little amount of money. The woman wants to know why the insurance company is offering so

---

7 Roger Fisher & William Ury, *Getting to Yes: Negotiating Agreement Without Giving In*, rev ed (New York, NY: Penguin Books, 2011) at 3–15.

8 This example is a modified version of an example taken from the book written by Roger Fisher & William Ury, *ibid* at 92–95.

little and is asking for $75,000, which would enable the woman to purchase a comparable second-hand, high-end, car. The insurance agent maintains that the amount requested is far too much and increases the company's offer by only $5,000.

Despite repeated questions as to basis for the sum of money that the company is prepared to pay, the insurance agent reiterates the company's last offer, saying that the amount offered corresponds with the company's usual compensation package.

The woman does not understand the reason given and asks that the agent check the red book, which provides the average prices of used cars. The insurance agent indicates that a three-year-old Mercedes. would sell for $65,000. This is the same model as the woman's car. However, the woman insists a higher amount is warranted because of the excellent condition of the car and the fact that the mileage of the Mercedes was only 20,000 kilometers. The woman maintains that the car was *like new*.

Finally, admitting that the mileage was extremely low, and that the woman's car was in better condition than the usual vehicle of that age, the agent increases the insurance company's offer to $70,000. Ultimately, the parties settle at $72,000.

In this example, had the parties continued to argue on position, in all probability, there would be a stalemate The introduction of an objective standard changed the dynamics between the parties and allowed for a reasonable outcome, rather than an arbitrary one.

Showing that you are prepared to collaborate in helping your clients reach an agreement does not mean that the opposite party will obtain whatever they want or that you will not assist your clients in obtaining the best possible result for them. When the focus is on the parties' interests and needs, there is a good chance that both parties will obtain satisfaction.

In a case of dismissal, where negotiations are focused on positions, the negotiations would revolve around the amount of compensation the employee is seeking. However, in collaborative negotiation, there are several possibilities that could satisfy an employee who no longer has a job. These include providing the employee with an outsourcing program, retraining, a letter of recommendation, help in preparing a curriculum vitae, assistance in finding another job, or help in setting up the employee's own business. If these interests and needs are satisfied, it is likely that the monetary aspect of the employee's claim will be more easily satisfied than if the parties negotiate on position.

Another way of reaching a settlement in collaborative negotiations is by increasing the number of possible options. Negotiations that are based on positions will often reach an impasse with each party believing that *either I get what I want*, or *you get what you want*. Put differently, each party assumes that one party wins and the other loses. However, both parties can gain in collaborative negotiations. It is useful to generate several potential options for settlement that are of mutual benefit and allow both parties to feel satisfied with the result. One example of such an option is the provision of an item that is of low cost to one party but of high interest to the other party.

There are, however, situations where positional bargaining is acceptable. Such cases typically involve parties who have had no ongoing relationship with each other and have no desire to continue to deal with each other. Other cases include those where the issue is not complex and there is no interest in spending any significant amount of time expressing emotions or finding the interests that will satisfy both sides. If the stakes are important but the relationship is not important, confrontation or competition is not a bad approach. An example of such an approach would be the case involving the purchase of an item where the only issue between the parties is the price of the item.

However, even in the above-mentioned example, the price is often not necessarily the sole issue to be settled. The parties could negotiate the timing of the payment and whether it will be paid in totality in one payment or payable in several instalments over time. In the latter case, the parties can determine the amount payable in each instalment, together with any interest that may be applied.

The more important the relationship is for the parties, the more a collaborative approach, based on interests and needs, should be favoured.

### 3) Initial Comments

After hearing the facts as perceived by the parties, and after establishing the interests and needs of the parties, when possible, mediators will try to elicit the parties' participation by asking them how they believe they can settle their conflict. Some mediators will allow the lawyers to put forward various proposals on behalf of their clients, while others will ask the respective lawyers to take a back seat and let their clients present their proposals.

The following comments, which are very constructive, should be presented either by you but preferably by your clients at the outset of the negotiations:

- Indicate that you believe that you have a strong case, but you are most interested in reaching a settlement and are willing to make certain compromises to resolve the existing conflict.
- Do not use legal jargon. It is preferable to use everyday language, since the other party may not have full comprehension of the legal terms involved in a case.
- State that there are disputed facts and that despite the lack of agreement and the respective differences between the parties, you are nevertheless open to the discussions that are about to take place. You wish to find the means of resolving the conflict.

The following behaviour should be adopted:

- Try to maintain a sympathetic approach, irrespective of the circumstances. The opposite party will be far more receptive to anything you say if you are open to listening to their position and proposals, as opposed to being aggressive and threatening. In fact, any attempt to threaten the other party will necessarily result in strong resentment and could potentially bring the mediation to a halt.
- Similarly, avoid name calling, even when the other party is not acting in good faith. There is no benefit in insulting the opposing party; consequently, you must also be polite in your comments. Negative statements will never help the discussions.

The following are typical comments and advice that mediators will present:

- Several issues are in dispute; try to resolve them one at a time.
- Consider presenting several possible proposals.
- Any suggestions you make are not in any way final, or the ones that will necessarily be adopted, but are merely options to be considered.
- Think outside the box; that is, be creative in presenting possible solutions to end your conflict and consider options that are not necessarily monetary.
- Do not immediately reject any suggestions, but at least consider the proposals.
- Either party can begin presenting suggestions for settling.

There are no formal rules to this part of the mediation, which involves ongoing proposals, counter proposals, and discussions in an attempt by the parties to resolve the issues between them. The negotiations usually begin with the parties remaining together in the same room. They will separate in a caucus when needed, as will be described in more detail in Section 14, below.

### 4) The Order of the Discussions

The order of discussion must be determined before negotiations begin.

When various issues exist in the conflict, there may be an evident or a rational order regarding the subjects to be discussed. In other cases, each issue may have the same importance for both or one of the parties.

For example, in the case of a latent defect involving mould, the lawsuit may list damages related to removal of the mould, the cost of alternate housing, medical expenses, and reconstruction of the affected part of the premises. In this instance, all the subjects may be listed and dealt with one at a time.

If the subjects are not all of equal importance, it is generally preferable to begin with the one that is the least controversial. If one subject is settled quickly, it provides a certain amount of momentum that encourages the parties to continue making progress.

Nothing prevents you from indicating what issue you would like to begin with first, particularly if your clients are prepared to make some initial concession on that item. This will show their good faith and their intent on reaching an agreement. You may also have considered an opening position. In fact, it is important for both your clients and the opposing party to come to the mediation session with several ideas and suggestions for settlement.

### 5) Presenting the First Proposal

It is not unusual for both parties to remain silent at the outset. Neither party wants to take the first step in showing their hand. Often, each party prefers to hear what the other party suggests as an opening proposal, in the hope that the other party will show how they intend to approach the negotiations. Then they can reject the proposal or present a counteroffer. When no one makes a move, a caucus is usually held. If neither party has presented a proposal even after a caucus is held, the mediator will often call upon one of the parties to start. It is necessary for one of the parties to make an offer for the mediation to proceed.

Who begins the negotiations? There is not total consensus on this question. Some authors hold that the plaintiffs are the ones who should present the first proposal. Others contend the defendants should present an offer first. Still others believe it does not matter who starts the process. However, the prevailing view is that the plaintiffs are the ones who should set out what they want, since the plaintiffs instituted the lawsuit and have already crunched the numbers in their claim. Defendants rarely like to make the first offer.[9]

9 Sheldon Stark, "Managing Opening Offers: Arriving at the Mediation Table" *International Academy of Mediators* (29 January 2021), online: https://iamed.org/archive/managing-opening-offers-arriving-at-the-mediation-table-part-2-of-3/.

You and your clients have discussed what your clients are hoping to achieve by means of the mediation. The question is, what is the starting point?

Parties who institute a lawsuit or a complaint often begin with the conclusions of their lawsuit, or their demand letter. The recipients often begin with the position adopted in their defence, or in their response to the demand letter. How each party has evaluated their respective position may be useful for litigation, but it is not helpful for mediation.

A proposal will generally lead to a counter proposal by the opposing party, who will respond in a similar way. Accordingly, when the plaintiffs begin with an excessively high amount, in all probability the defendants will reply with an excessively low amount. If the plaintiffs then reduce their claim by exceedingly small amounts and the defendants increase their offers by similar small amounts, mirroring their increases by the amount of the plaintiffs' decreases, the parties will spend hours at the mediation, with little progress.[10] A great deal of time is wasted. Therefore, consider the effect that your clients' proposal will have on the other party's potential counter proposal.

The first proposal should be credible. Such a proposal has more likeliness to induce the opposing party to do the same. Exceedingly high offers by plaintiffs or exceedingly low offers by defendants not only impede progress but are seen as unreasonable. A proper starting point for plaintiffs is a proposal that is sufficiently high but is still serious and shows credibility. It will set the tone while at the same time providing the plaintiffs with a negotiating margin and the possibility to settle at an acceptable amount.[11]

---

10 Wolters Kluwer, "Offers in Mediation, Busting the Myths" *Kluwer Mediation Blog* (5 May 2022), online: https://mediationblog.kluwerarbitration.com/2022/05/05/offers-in-mediation-busting-the-myths.

11 Bruce M. Brusavich, "A Mediation Primer for the Plaintiff's Attorney" *Plaintiff Magazine* (September 2015), online: https://plaintiffmagazine.com/images/issues/2015/09-september/reprints/Brusavich_A-mediation-primer-for-the-plaintiffs-attorney_Plaintiff-magzine.pdf.

A useful rule of thumb for plaintiffs is to begin by proposing an amount that is less than what your clients stated in their lawsuit, if your clients are the plaintiffs, but more than the net amount that they can hope to get if the case goes to court. The amount your clients propose can also be a strong indication as to their desire to settle.

Take, for example, the case of a hidden defect discovered in a home your clients purchased. They had the repairs evaluated. The cost would come to $300,000, and you have made a claim in your clients' lawsuit for this amount. If they begin the negotiations by saying that if they went to court, they would be asking for $300,000, but are willing to reduce the amount they are seeking to $275,000 in order to settle, the defendants understand that a certain amount of flexibility can be expected. The defendants will also understand that your clients are interested in making a deal.

Frequently, the defendants will begin with an excessively low offer, with the hope that the plaintiffs will drop their claim and the parties will settle somewhere in the middle. However, when the defendants make an offer that is excessively low, they are seen as being lacking credibility. This is not a useful way to begin any settlement discussions. It is preferable for the defendants to start with a reasonable and legitimate proposal and continue negotiations in a fair manner, in the same way the plaintiffs did.

The party who begins the negotiations often sets the tone for the ensuing offers. How will the first proposal be perceived? Is the party being reasonable or unreasonable? How realistic is the proposal? Is that party realistic, or have they over evaluated the chances of succeeding if the case goes to court? Has the party making the first offer taken into consideration the risks involved in a trial, including the disputed facts in the case, contradictions in the version of facts presented, or other weaknesses in the case?

What is important is the presentation of a credible proposal and one whose basis you can explain, as for example, the market cost of the repairs that are needed for the material damage your clients have suffered, the moral damages that the court has granted in similar cases of personal injury, or the usual sharing of parents' visiting rights during the holiday season in divorce cases. Consequently, when presenting the proposal, advise your clients to indicate the basis for what they are requesting or offering, as, for example, *We are asking for X because of* (state the reason for requesting X). This will require the other party to consider not only the proposal but also the reasoning behind it.

In both the first and subsequent proposals, it is useful to be clear as to what exactly the offer entails. Is it simply a sum of money? Will interest be added? Will the amount be subject to tax or not? Will it be payable in instalments? While initial proposals often do not deal with such issues, keep them in mind for ongoing proposals.

It is also advisable to indicate that the figure or proposal advanced is not etched in stone; rather you expect the opposing party to respond with a reasonable proposal. If either party adopts a rigid position at the outset, it will in all probability have a negative impact, such that the other party will also adopt a rigid position and an impasse will occur.

It often happens that the parties are unable to offer any option whatsoever at the outset. When neither party presents a proposal and both remain silent, the process will not begin. This is the opportune time for a caucus to take place.

The same applies when the offers and counteroffers stop early on and both parties are unwilling to present any additional proposals. An impasse occurs. In such circumstances, generally both parties will ask to meet privately with their lawyers to discuss the next offers they plan to make.

Mediators typically ask for the caucus, but nothing prevents you from asking for a caucus even if no one has made this request. The subject of impasses will be discussed in more detail in Section 16.

### 6) Presenting Several Proposals

Parties often put forward a single proposal, namely a proposal dealing with a monetary figure. They talk about what they are prepared to pay or what they are prepared to accept. This is the typical approach in positional bargaining.

A better approach is to put forward as many proposals as possible, rather than trying to narrow the gap between the two positions. The point is not to propose a solution that the other side must accept or reject. You should advise your clients to present and discuss multiple proposals without immediately deciding on any of them. In doing this, it is important to emphasize that a proposal is exactly that: a possibility for consideration.

In presenting a proposal, one useful way of proceeding is to group different possibilities of an option together, such as tying a monetary proposal to the timing of the payment. For example, a certain sum could be paid over an extended period, or another lesser amount could be offered if the payment is to be made immediately.

Consider a case of damages. Rather than have your clients argue over how much they are asking for to have the damage repaired and how much the other party is willing to pay, a better approach would be for both parties to choose an independent contractor who would evaluate the damage and provide an opinion as to the actual cost of the repairs.

Alternatively, your clients should suggest that two evaluations be conducted, and an average be taken of the two. Further proposals could centre around who will perform the work, when the repairs will take place, and finally what amount the defendants will contribute to the project.

In the case of a dispute over the payment of dividends in a company owned by two persons, rather than argue over the amount of compensation that should be paid, a more beneficial approach would be for the parties to renegotiate the terms of their partnership agreement, with an understanding that all decisions will be joint ones. The parties can together select a lawyer who would draft a revised agreement which the parties could use to determine all future arrangements between them. Once the parties reach an agreement on the parameters for future dealings, there is a greater possibility of resolving the current issue.

### 7) Reacting to Proposals of the Other Party

Often, when one side presents a proposal, the other side reacts strongly, either criticizing or immediately rejecting it. The same occurs when the other side presents their proposal. This pattern goes back and forth and becomes a battle of force, with each side digging into their pre-established position.

To avoid this clash, it is important for your clients not to attack, but to consider how they can bring their interests, and those of the opposing party, into play. There are various ways of handling this situation. Consider the following examples.

If the other party is angry or upset, there is less likelihood that they will collaborate. In such circumstances, try to reduce the emotional level by a positive approach. Your clients could say:

We understand you are angry about .... We cannot change the past, but we hope that together we can find a way forward and resolve our conflict.

If the proposal advanced by the opposite party is unrealistic or outrageous, your clients should ask:

How would you feel if you were in our place? Would you consider the proposal acceptable?

If the proposition presented is far from what your clients consider to be acceptable, look for the basis of the proposal and how it can be improved. Your clients can begin by showing that they have listened to what the other side has said and understand their position. Instead of attacking the proposition, they can respond by talking about other options. As an example, your clients could say:

Your proposal is a possibility, but perhaps we should look for other possible solutions that will be satisfactory for all of us.

Your clients could also ask questions about the position that the other party has put forward, which allows the opposing party to elaborate on their proposal. For example, your clients could ask:

You believe that ... is true. Is our understanding correct?

Asking questions is an appropriate tool for your clients to use, rather than attacking or repeating their own position or statements. It provides the other side with the opportunity to reflect, explain what they mean, and confront the issue. For example, your clients could say:

We hear what you are saying, but would you be willing to consider X?

If we removed our demand for X, would you agree to Y?

If we offered X, would you then consider our proposal?

What if we looked at the problem from a different perspective?

If the other party says they refuse to pay more, your clients could ask for their reasons. For example, your clients could say:

Please explain the reasons for your refusal.

Your offer is far below the cost of the damages (or the market value or what the courts would award), so please explain why you are offering so little.

Given the cost to repair (or the market value), what makes the amount you are offering fair?

Given the cost to repair (or the market value), why should we accept your offer?

Still another response is to ask how the problem can be resolved:

How can we carry out the necessary repairs with such a small amount of money?

Alternatively, your clients could suggest that the other party modify their offer by including an item or a service that is of interest to your clients. In the case of damages and the need for repairs, your clients could ask that the other party improve the offer by saying:

Your offer is still somewhat low. Would you consider including the services of an engineer (or an architect) in your proposal?

We understand that you do not want to pay more, but would you be willing to add additional benefits to our (insurance) policy?

Similarly, when the opposite party reacts negatively to proposals put forward by your clients, it is important that your clients not respond in a hostile manner. Accordingly, when the opposite side disagrees with a solution put forward by your clients and rejects it outright, rather than repeating the proposal and defending it, reacting in a hostile manner, or criticizing the other party, your clients could ask the opposing party for their input and to provide a solution by saying:

What do you suggest?

How would you resolve this issue if you were in our place?

Asking for help from the opposing party can bring about their collaboration in trying to find a solution.

If the other party attacks your clients, it is not helpful for your clients to respond in kind. Rather, they should tell the other party that their approach is not constructive:

We hear that you are angry, but we are not going to resolve our dispute if you call us names. Remember, we are supposed to be civil with each other.

If your clients are upset about statements made by the other party, rather than condemning the opposing party, it is more persuasive for your clients to indicate the impact the other party's words had on them. For example, your clients could respond by saying:

We felt hurt and betrayed when you said that ... rather than: What you said about us was false and offensive.

### 8) Reframing

When listening to statements made by the other party that are counterproductive to reaching an agreement, a good method for your clients to use is that of reformulating or reframing. It allows the parties to move away from their positions and acknowledge their interests and needs. There are several ways of applying reframing.

Reframing can be used to clarify a statement that was made or better understand what was said. For example, your clients can ask:

Do we understand that . . .

Are you saying that . . . ? Please tell us if we are wrong.

Can you tell us why you want that?

Help us understand your proposal. What makes that fair?

Reframing can also neutralize toxic or insulting language by eliminating the inflammatory words. When the other party states that your clients have lied to them, your clients should respond by turning an offensive statement into a positive one. The following is an example of neutralizing toxic language:

We understand that since we have given you inaccurate information in the past, you are hesitant to rely on our statements now.

Reframing can also modify perceptions and show that you understood what the other party has said. For example, if the opposite party perceived a situation differently from that of your clients, your clients could offer the following response:

We are sorry that we caused you to feel embarrassment; it was not our intention.

We think you misunderstood us. That was not what we meant.

You may have a point, but how can we rectify this?

Reframing can also contribute to resolving the conflict by putting the emphasis on common goals. For example, in response to a proposal that is not feasible, rather than say that such a proposal is out of the question, your clients could say:

We seem to have contrary positions. How do you suggest that we deal with this issue together, so that all of us can be comfortable with the potential solution?

The language used in responding to the opposite party is important. Reframing what the other party has said can reduce and neutralize a heated exchange. Avoiding criticism and offensive language is essential. Asking for explanations, expressing understanding, responding in a positive manner, seeking further options, and asking for help or input are all means of reducing tensions and increasing collaboration, which are necessary in trying to reach a settlement.

## 9) Who Is Deciding on the Opposite Side?

The decision as to the content of a settlement in mediation belongs to the parties. In many cases, the persons who instituted the action know how much compensation or what alternatives they are prepared to accept to resolve the conflict. The defendants also know how much they are prepared to pay or what alternatives they are willing to offer.

However, in many situations, each party will turn to their lawyer for advice and suggestions concerning the proposals they should advance. The parties feel that their lawyers, having a legal background, can guide them with respect to appropriate offers. They are aware that their lawyers have a better idea than they do of the potential outcome of the case in court, if the parties do not settle in mediation.

It is important to determine who is making the decisions on the opposite side. Is the party deciding, or is the lawyer the one who is deciding, or both? The same applies to the situation where the plaintiffs or the defendants are a couple, or where the other party consists of several people. The importance of this determination lies in knowing who your clients must try to persuade.

When both the lawyer and the clients on the opposite side are on the same page, identifying who is deciding makes little difference. The challenge arises when the other party and their lawyer have different views on the conflict and on its solution. When clients are the ones who are clearly controlling the negotiations and are being difficult by showing little flexibility or by objecting to any proposal that is put forward, you should suggest a meeting, in private, with that party's lawyer.

There is no guarantee that either the party or their lawyer will accept this suggestion. Even if they both agree, there is no guarantee that this proposal will produce any results. It is nevertheless worthwhile to suggest that such a meeting take place. This will allow you to discuss the situation with the opposing lawyer, with the hope that the lawyer will talk to their clients and attempt to obtain more collaborative behaviour.

A more complicated scenario occurs when the clients and their lawyer do not see eye to eye and the difficulty in negotiating stems from the position adopted by the opposing lawyer. One such scenario occurs when clients clearly want to settle their conflict and their lawyer is creating an impediment to the process, even suggesting that it will be better to go to court. In this type of situation, the best approach is to ask for a caucus and then point out the problem to the mediator, who in all probability has already noticed the situation and will hopefully caucus with the other party to resolve the difference between the clients and their lawyer.

Another means of dealing with such a situation is a private meeting between the parties without the lawyers. Since a mediator is not supposed to intervene in a client-attorney relationship, as counsel, you can suggest that the mediator arrange for a meeting between the parties alone, provided that the opposing attorney agrees. Alternatively, you could ask the lawyer representing the other party to allow the parties to talk to each other in private. By removing the person who is counterproductive, you increase the chance of reaching a settlement. This, of course, is possible only if the opposing lawyer agrees and the parties are on speaking terms. Situations where a meeting between parties can be fruitful are set out in Section 16(f), below.

### 10) The Style of the Person Who Is Deciding

Once you have determined who is the one deciding on the opposing side, it is equally important to also determine their negotiating style.

Are they very formal or relatively casual? Are they emotional, or are they not demonstrating any feelings? Are they open and transparent, or are they keeping their true position hidden? Do they mean what they say? Are they more outgoing than your clients, or are they timid? Are they cautious or impetuous? Are they flexible or rigid in their discussions? Do they want everything put into writing, or are they willing to deal with proposals orally?

The more your clients' approach is the same or similar to that of the other party, the easier the negotiations will be. When the style of your clients and the other party are totally different, either party may feel ill at ease. A person who is very shy may feel uncomfortable with an extremely outgoing person. Similarly, a person who is very emotional may have difficulty dealing with someone who is restrained, impassive, and hides their feelings.

You cannot change your clients' personalities. At best, you can try to intervene, when possible, to help your clients deal with given situations. For example, if your clients are very formal, you can have your clients express their reactions in a polite way, such as *We would appreciate it if you called us Mr. Smith and Mrs. Smith rather than Joe and Mary.*

If your clients are very shy and cautious, you could ask them if they want to respond right away or whether they prefer to think about the proposal. You can also ask for a caucus to assure your clients that they do not have to respond immediately and do not have to feel intimidated, since you will help them in considering the proposals.

On the other hand, if your clients are extremely outgoing and open but the opposing party is very shy and not readily transparent, you can request a caucus. There, you should caution your clients to try not to overwhelm the opposing party.

### 11) How Quickly Should an Agreement Be Reached?

There are no rules as to how much time a mediation should take. However, a word of caution. Even when the matter will resolve quickly, it is important for some negotiation to take place between the parties before any deal is reached. A pitfall to be avoided in negotiations occurs when one party at the negotiating table overbids, in an attempt to achieve a settlement, and subsequently regrets the proposal.

Consider the following example. The plaintiff has claimed $300,000 in a lawsuit. The mediation begins and the defendant offers the plaintiff $200,000. If the plaintiff immediately accepts that offer, the defendant will be upset, believing that considerably less could have been offered. The defendant will most likely be very dissatisfied.

This phenomenon, where a party offers too much and the first proposition is readily accepted by the other party, has been described as the *winner's curse*.[12]

Neither party wants to feel that they have lost in the negotiations. Both parties need to reject at least one proposal made by the other party. Following these initial rejections of any proposal made by the opposing party, the true discussions can begin, with the resulting give and take of successive proposals. After the parties attempt to achieve their objective, the result that they ultimately agree on has a good chance of being acceptable to both parties.

### 12) The Pace of the Negotiations

Different parties have different ways of negotiating. Some are prepared to immediately deal with the issue and are not interested in spending hours inching their way toward a settlement.

Others, on the other hand, feel uncomfortable by moving rapidly and are afraid of making concessions too quickly. They would rather first see what position the other party has adopted and how much they are prepared to modify their position with each new proposal.

12 Program on Negotiation staff, "Definition of the Winner's Curse in Negotiations" Program on Negotiation, Harvard Law School Daily Blog (13 October 2020), online: www.pon.harvard.edu/daily/negotiation-skills-daily/identifying-the-winners-curse-in-negotiation.

When both parties have the same approach, whether their pace is quick or slow, the negotiations work well. An example of this type of situation occurs when both parties are aware of what they foresee as the proper outcome, and both put forward reasonable and realistic proposals and then move quickly toward an acceptable agreement.

It becomes more difficult when one of the parties is anxious to get to the heart of the problem right away and put a final amount on the table, while the other party needs to take a more cautious approach and move gradually toward a consensus, little by little. If your clients' approach is to move rapidly to resolve the conflict but you see that the other party is more reluctant to act in the same way and constantly takes breaks to confer with their lawyer, you should advise your clients to slow their pace. If not, the more cautious party will feel pressured and may become even more cautious. Moreover, if your clients move too quickly, they may also find that they have compromised more than the other party at an early stage of the process.

Conversely, if it is the other party who is moving quickly to reach an agreement while your clients are more prudent and want to take their time to consider every proposal, you may find that the opposite party stops making any further concessions. Alternatively, the opposite party may try to push your clients into an uncomfortable position, demanding that they react faster than they are prepared to do. In such a situation, you must be aware of your clients' needs and provide the necessary support for their slow pace, requesting caucuses if necessary.

### 13) The Interests and Needs of the Opposite Party

During the entire process, it is opportune for you to try to determine what are the interests of the other party. Put differently, what are their main concerns and needs.

Is the opponent concerned about their reputation? Is confidentiality an important aspect? Is a trial to be avoided at all costs? Is financial compensation most important? Are there other equally important options or options that are even more important than financial compensation?

You can attempt to arrive at some understanding of what would satisfy the opposite party by listening to their version of the facts, listening to their emotions, and having your clients ask appropriate questions during the negotiations.

If you can determine what the principal concerns are of the other party, you must then try to establish how they can be addressed, whether they correspond in any way with the interests of your clients, and whether your clients can meet them.

Establishing the interests and needs of the opposite party will be of great assistance in trying to find some common ground and reach an agreement that is acceptable to both your clients and the other party. Even when each side is seeking a different outcome, a satisfactory agreement is still possible, provided that each party obtains a solution that meets their interests and needs.

The possibility of non-monetary proposals should not be forgotten. Often, such proposals are a means of reaching a settlement when the monetary aspect is insufficient. Such proposals include an apology, a letter of recommendation, a supply of goods, the provision of services, and so on.

### 14) Caucuses

As already indicated, the caucus is a private meeting that takes place between the mediator, and you and your client, during the mediation process. The other party and their lawyer are not present. Whatever is said or whatever information is provided in the caucus will not be disclosed to the other party unless you give the mediator permission to do so.

The caucus is an essential aspect of the process. It allows each of the parties the opportunity to freely review the issues, discuss their concerns with the mediator, and show their emotions without the fear of compromising their position with respect to the opposing party.

The caucus has many purposes. Amongst them is the possibility for you, your clients, or the other party to:

- Make an offer.
- Consider an offer.
- Let off steam.
- Regain composure.
- Deal with aggressive, intimidating, or threatening behaviour from the other party.
- Be open.
- Obtain clarification of an issue.
- Obtain information that may lead to other options.
- Consider alternative proposals or raise new ideas.
- Do a reality check or objectively evaluate your clients' case.
- Reassess your clients' position.
- Encourage your clients to modify their position.
- Discuss the risks of not settling and going to trial.
- Discuss your clients' concerns.
- Discuss the benefits of settling.
- Re-evaluate your negotiation strategy.
- Provide the mediator with your clients' offers or position.
- Speak confidentially with the mediator.
- Provide the mediator with your clients' bottom line.

Although it is the mediator who usually suggests a caucus and holds as many caucuses as often as deemed necessary, you can also request that the mediator hold a caucus with you and your clients. If needed, you can also request that you and your clients meet on your own, without the mediator. Mediators will rarely refuse such a request.

While you have explained the nature of the caucus to your clients when you outlined how the mediation session proceeds, it is also necessary to consider when you will ask for a caucus.

Generally, there is not a set formula or an exact moment for caucuses to take place. They usually occur when neither party has provided any indication as to how they envisage a settlement and no proposals have been put forward. They also take place when an offer has been made and the other lawyer and the opposing party wish to discuss the offer in private, with the assistance of the mediator. In this case, the lawyer will request a caucus, if the mediator has not already done so.

Other instances include inappropriate behaviour on the part of either party, distraught emotions, impasses when both parties no longer wish to make any concessions, and the need to discuss your clients' reactions to pending offers, as well as simply the desire to take a break to consider strategy.

Finally, there are situations where the parties have such a dislike for each other that they do not want to be in the same room. This situation obliges the mediator to go back and forth between them and present each party with the position and proposals of the other party.

### a) To Make an Offer

One of the first uses of a caucus occurs when neither party has made a first offer. You may, at this point, consider a meeting with your clients to discuss your starting point. This can occur whether your clients are the plaintiffs or the defendants.

The parties are usually told by their lawyers that they should come to a mediation session with several proposals in mind, together with an idea of their starting point in negotiations. Despite these instructions, each party is often reluctant to be the first to present an offer. When this situation occurs or when other issues listed below need to be discussed with your clients, you should ask the mediator for a caucus.

If there is more than one issue in dispute, or more than one aspect of a case listed in a lawsuit, you may wish to discuss which issue to begin with, generally selecting one where there is a possibility of consensus.

If your clients are the ones who instituted the proceedings, you would discuss how much they are willing to decrease the initial amount claimed in the lawsuit or demand letter as well as whether they are prepared to present their position first.

If your clients are the defendants, you would discuss whether they are willing to present an offer before hearing the plaintiffs' position as to how much they are claiming. In both instances, your discussion should entail whether any non-monetary proposals can be put forward.

As already stated, most mediators feel that plaintiffs should begin the process. However, it is immaterial who begins with a proposal. On the other hand, it may set the tone and flow of the negotiations. You may consider it opportune for your clients to indicate, by a first proposal, whether the amount indicated in their lawsuit or defence is close to what they are still seeking.

These are subjects that you and your clients should have discussed prior to the mediation session. However, even when you have talked about these issues beforehand with your clients, it is not unusual for your clients to want to consult you at the mediation itself before they present any proposal to the other party.

### b) To Consider an Offer

Some clients are comfortable considering an offer or a proposal in the presence of the opposite party. They immediately respond with a counteroffer, particularly if they have decided how quickly they wish to negotiate.

However, more often than not, your clients will prefer meeting with you after an offer has been made by the opposite party. They will usually want to discuss their response with you, before responding to the proposal.

A meeting with your clients in private, or together with the mediator, will allow you to guide your clients in evaluating the seriousness of the other party's proposal and to determine how your clients should react to it. You may suggest that your clients reject the opponent's position outright and maintain their previous position, that they should modify their previous proposal to a greater or lesser extent and present a counter proposal, or that they should present a completely alternative proposal.

### c) To Let off Steam

Your clients may become extremely angry when hearing an allegation of the other party that they consider to be false. They may begin to raise their voice, argue heatedly, or use inappropriate language.

This is an appropriate time to ask for a caucus or simply take a break. Although it is understandable that a false statement can provoke anger, you should, in private, remind your clients that even if they vehemently disagree with the other party's position, they will not succeed in reaching any sort of agreement if they are hostile to that party. Accordingly, the caucus provides the possibility for your clients to let off steam and calm down before returning to the plenary session.

### d) To Regain Composure

Your clients may become upset during the mediation for any number of reasons. These range from reacting to a statement they find insulting to reliving a situation in which they suffered pain or humiliation. A client who is overcome with emotion may be on the verge of tears or begin to cry.

Your clients will not wish to display these reactions in front of the other party. To do so would be embarrassing. A caucus allows your clients to deal with overwhelming emotions and regain composure in private.

The caucus also provides your clients with an opportunity to openly discuss their feelings. In addition, it provides you (and the mediator) with information that can be particularly useful:

- Were you aware that your clients felt these emotions?
- Have your clients' feelings been fully expressed such that the other party is aware of the impact of their words or actions?
- Is it opportune to inform the other party of the emotions that your clients had not divulged during their presentation of their story?
- Can your clients generate some empathy by informing the other party of their feelings, which could potentially help in modifying the other party's position?

These and other such questions can be discussed during a break from the plenary session.

#### e) To Deal with Aggressive Behaviour

Your clients may lash out if they are provoked by statements made by the opposite party. They may blurt out their frustration and become aggressive simply by reacting to what was said to them. Their aggression toward the other party can easily result in a counter reaction. The other party could also respond in anger or even threaten to leave.

Asking for a caucus is essential if such a situation arises. It is necessary to discuss your clients' conduct toward the opposing party. No agreement can be achieved if your clients act aggressively.

It is useful to remind your clients, in a caucus, that it is not in their interest to maintain their aggression and that if they want to settle the conflict, they will succeed more easily with honey than with vinegar. You can advise them that if they fail to change their behaviour, it is likely that the other party will leave the mediation. It is evident that if that occurs, there will no longer be any chance of settling their case.

Once your clients accept that they must act in a civil manner and carry out a rational discussion, they should be encouraged to return to the plenary session, apologize for their behaviour, and continue the discussions.

#### f) To Deal with Intimidating or Threatening Behaviour from the Other Party

There are times when it is necessary for the parties to be separated from each other. It is important to ask for a caucus if the other party's behaviour becomes intimidating to your clients. You would necessarily want your clients to be in a separate room with the assurance that the mediator will deal with the situation. There is no justification for your clients to feel uncomfortable in any way during the mediation.

However, remember that if the other party threatens to pursue their lawsuit, this is not a threat that should cause alarm. It may be a negotiating tactic, or it may simply indicate that the opposing party does not really have the goal of settling, in which case you may wish to adjust your approach accordingly.

If, on the other hand, the threats are of a more serious nature, you should ask the mediator to intervene and remind the parties of their obligation to be civil with each other and to refrain from intimidation, threatening language, or threatening behaviour.

### g) To Be Open

Your clients may not wish to share information with the opposite party if they believe it can be detrimental to their own case. However, they may be amenable to discussing such information with the mediator in a caucus because that is a confidential process.

During the caucus, your clients can discuss any aspect of their case with you and with the mediator. They can be completely honest and open with respect to any information divulged, since it will not be revealed to the other party unless you give the mediator permission to do so. Such information may, for example, relate to your clients' fear of going to trial, their concern about the impact the stress will have on their health, or other facts that limit their negotiating strategy with the opponent.

The caucus not only provides a protective screen for your clients but also provides the mediator with information that most often is useful. It assists the mediator in evaluating the respective positions of each party and helps the mediator to fully act as a facilitator.

### h) To Obtain Clarification of an Issue

You may also want to use the caucus to clarify an issue that has arisen. There, you can ask the mediator, without the presence of the other party, any number of questions about statements the other party has made or proposals that the other party has suggested. Questions can include:

What is the basis for the amount offered by the other party?

What was the basis for refusing an offer my clients made?

What did the other party mean by saying . . . ?

Can the other party substantiate the claims they made?

Do you think the other party can improve upon the last proposal?

It is not unusual to make assumptions about matters when we do not have all the facts, or we do not fully understand what was said. Therefore, it is useful to obtain all the explanations that are needed to be able to deal with an issue appropriately.

### i) To Obtain Information that May Lead to Other Options

It is not unusual for the give and take of proposals to slow considerably during the process, with little hope that more movement will be forthcoming. The caucus allows you to confer with the mediator and ask if there is any information that could be shared with you that would help you in making other proposals of interest to the other party or that would induce that party to settle.

For example, if you represent the defendants, you could ask the mediator to find out from the opposite party:

- whether a monetary package is the only option for settlement, and if so,
- how much more must be offered to close the deal, or
- whether there is something else that would be of interest to the opposite party and which they would consider as part of a settlement, such as the provision of a service, equipment, or assistance of a particular nature.

If you are representing the plaintiffs, you could ask the mediator:

- whether the opposite party will meet your clients' bottom line, or
- whether the other party is prepared to acknowledge their mistake and apologize (or offer goods or a service that your clients want).

Although you could ask the other party such questions directly, you can avoid the confrontation that may ensue if the other party rejects a suggestion outright by raising these questions privately in a caucus.

### j) To Consider Alternate Proposals or to Raise New Ideas

Often, the parties come to a standstill. Neither party has moved from their last position. While you can always brainstorm in a plenary session, it is far more comfortable for your clients to meet with you and the mediator separately to try to figure out how to move forward.

During a caucus, you can suggest alternate propositions for settlement, or you can ask whether the mediator has any suggestions. It is easier to do so in private, where your clients can reject any ideas you may have and freely discuss new possibilities without the other party's knowledge as to the alternative options that you are considering.

### k) To Do a Reality Check or Objectively Evaluate Your Clients' Case

You have evaluated your clients' case and the chance for success in a trial before making a claim on their behalf or responding to an action. However, during the mediation you have had the possibility of hearing another side of the story.

The facts presented by the opposite party may differ somewhat from those stated in the legal proceedings. You and your clients may hear more detail, together with supporting evidence, about the conduct that has been alleged or statements that were made. The presentation by the other party may raise doubts about some of the facts your clients gave you or lead you to question the validity of these facts and of the position your clients have adopted.

The caucus provides you with an opportunity to do a reality check with respect to your clients' position and to consider whether or not their allegations are accurate.

### l) To Reassess Your Clients' Position

The caucus is the ideal moment to reassess your clients' position. You may have heard facts you had not dealt with before. The mediator may ask questions or raise issues that lead you to reassess your clients' claim.

Consider for example a claim you made on behalf of your clients, who suffered moral damages. If the mediator questions the amount your clients are seeking and asks you to review several cases dealing with the amount of compensation that has been granted by the courts, you may realize that your claim exceeds the maximum that has been awarded in recent years. You will understand that you will have little chance obtaining the compensation you are seeking on behalf of your clients if you go to trial. This consideration will impact your clients' claim in mediation as well.

New information, whether in fact or in law, can lead you to reassess your clients' position. Most parties prefer to rethink their position and their approach in a caucus, rather than in the presence of the opposite party.

#### m) To Encourage Your Clients to Modify Their Position

After doing a reality check and reassessing your clients' position, it may be time to encourage your clients to modify their claim or their defence. Probably, your clients have come to the mediation angry, distrustful of the opposite party, and vengeful. They have adopted a certain position, based on the facts they understood to be true.

During the mediation, they have had a chance to hear another version of the facts, including facts they were not aware of and scenarios they never contemplated. They have also been made aware that their case is not ironclad. They may begin to realize that they cannot achieve the outcome they hoped to achieve.

A caucus is the time to deal with such new facts. In the privacy of a caucus, you can review this information, discuss its impact, and the extent to which it could affect your clients' case. After you have reassessed your clients' situation, you should try to encourage them to be more flexible in their proposals.

#### n) To Discuss the Risks of Not Settling and Going to Trial

Some lawyers will tell their clients that any agreement that is acceptable to them is preferable to a judgment over which their clients have no control. No matter how good a case you believe you have, there is always a risk in going to trial.

The variables that can impact the outcome of your clients' case in court are numerous and include any one of the following, among others:

- The facts in the case are disputed, and you cannot be certain whose version the judge will find credible.
- The caselaw is divided with respect to the issue in litigation.
- You do not have the necessary evidence on all aspects of the case.
- The court has not assessed damages in the same way you have assessed them.
- Your clients will not testify well in court when examined.
- You are not assured that your witnesses will testify well in court.
- Your clients will not stand up well under cross-examination.
- You are not certain whether your expert witness will be effective.

It is important to point out to your clients the many variables that could affect their case. This type of discussion evidently should take place in a private meeting. The other party does not have to hear any doubts you may have about the potential outcome of your clients' case in court.

### o) To Discuss Your Clients' Concerns

Your clients may want to meet with you and the mediator, without the other party, for any one of various reasons. These reasons could include:

- their fears of going to trial
- the stress of the litigation and its impact on their well being
- their concerns about the mounting cost of the litigation
- whether they should alter their expectations in the mediation session to reach an agreement
- whether the other party is negotiating in good faith

- whether the other party is on a fishing expedition—that is, only attending mediation as a means of fishing for information that may be useful in court
- whether they will have to make more concessions to reach an agreement, and so on

It is evident that these and any other concerns are not meant for the other party to hear. In a caucus, you can discuss such issues freely with your clients so that they can return to the plenary and continue the discussions in a calm and confident manner.

### p) To Discuss the Benefits of Settling

There are usually several opportunities during the mediation for you to discuss with your clients the benefits of reaching an agreement rather than going to court and having a judgment imposed on them.

One benefit of a mediation is the possibility of reaching an agreement that is comprised of or includes a non-monetary item. In some cases, a non-monetary solution can be a preferred outcome and one that the court will not have jurisdiction to order. Your clients may find it more convenient to obtain a particular solution than a large sum of money.

Consider the case of homeowners who sued a seller for the water damage suffered after the buyers took possession of their home. A contractor had carried out repairs, but the homeowners' insurer refused to provide the homeowners with home insurance, pointing to the repeated leakage surrounding the chimney area of the house. The parties agreed to participate in a mediation to resolve the lawsuit.

Although the homeowners wanted money to cover the cost of their repairs, obtaining the insurance they needed was of greater interest to them than a limited amount of money for their damages.

Since the insurance company was aware of the past leakage and was concerned about further leakage and damage in the future, the seller agreed to hire an engineer to carry out an inspection. After assessing the work that had been done, the engineer concluded that the repairs met existing standards and there would be no further leaks in the foreseeable future.

The engineer agreed to provide the insurance company with a report. The report would include the engineer's professional opinion and advise the company of the results of the evaluation. On this basis, the insurance company was prepared to reinstate the insurance for the home. Once the issue of insurance coverage was resolved, the parties easily reached an agreement on the amount of damages to be paid.

Even when your clients' goal is solely to obtain a monetary settlement, if an agreement is reached with respect to an amount that your clients find acceptable, they will usually obtain the funds immediately following the settlement, or within a short period of time. This differs significantly from the delays involved in getting a court date, waiting for the judgment to be rendered, and facing the possibility of further delays if an appeal is instituted.

You should remind your clients that the outcome of a trial is never certain. In addition to the risks involved in presenting a case before the court, the costs for your clients will continue to rise, the stress associated with the process is ongoing, and the time involved both in preparing for trial and being present at court is considerable.

Accordingly, it is appropriate to tell your clients that unless the position of the opposite party is totally unacceptable, or unless you believe that the outcome from a judgment will necessarily be better than any settlement your clients can obtain, there are advantages to reaching an agreement with the other party.

### q) To Re-evaluate Your Negotiation Strategy

Before the mediation, you planned how you would proceed, what suggestions you would give to your clients with respect to their opening proposal, the pace of the negotiations, the offers on the table, and their choices for settlement.

However, unlike a courtroom, mediation has more room for the unexpected. At trial, there is a framework: the plaintiffs and witnesses are questioned by the plaintiffs' own lawyer and then cross-examined by the opposing lawyer. The defendants present their case in the same way. The plaintiffs can present counter proof, and then arguments by both parties ensue.

Mediations are less structured than a trial, and the discussions are not limited to what has been alleged in the court proceedings. The parties may delve into subjects that are indirectly related to the lawsuit, or even unrelated, but which are nevertheless important because they may deal with the parties' real interests.

It is usual for lawyers who specialize in litigation to be well prepared to avoid surprises during trials. Mediation, on the other hand, does not necessarily allow for the same control of the process. The offers and the pace of proposals are sometimes difficult to predict. What transpires may not correspond to what you had planned at the outset.

This is one of the reasons that the caucus is so useful. It allows you to remove yourself from the ongoing discussions and reevaluate your negotiation strategy, including the following subjects:

- What should the next offer be?
- How quickly should your clients make any further concessions?
- What will induce the other party to offer more (or accept less)?
- What will happen if your clients maintain their position and remain unyielding?
- What non-monetary options can be proposed?
- Is the other party open to options that do not involve monetary compensation?

These and other questions can be considered with your clients in the privacy of the caucus.

#### r) To Provide the Mediator with Your Clients' Offers or Position

A meeting with the mediator in a caucus gives you a chance to inform the mediator of your clients' proposed offers while asking that this information not be divulged to the other party.

Meeting with the mediator privately and indicating where your clients stand with respect to the proposals on the table will allow the mediator to determine if there is a huge gap in the parties' positions; whether or not your proposal is reasonable; whether the parties are approaching a common solution; and whether you need to come up with an alternate proposal.

By providing the mediator with information as to your clients' next proposal, the mediator will be able to give you some input with respect to your strategy.

As an example, the mediator may point out that the opposite party has conceded several times, while your clients have not done so, and that unless your clients are willing to sweeten their offer (if they are the defendants) or accept less (if they are the plaintiffs), there is little likelihood of an agreement.

In short, the information the mediator conveys will allow you to determine whether or not you should suggest that your clients adopt a more compromising position.

### s) To Speak Confidentially with the Mediator

The caucus is an opportune time to discuss any matter with the mediator in confidence. Your discussions can include discussing your clients' objectives, what amount of compensation your clients would find acceptable, and whether they are prepared to consider non-monetary options. The discussions could also encompass a proposal your clients think could be of interest to the other party and would like the mediator's opinion regarding the other party's likely receptiveness. It could be related to a concern that your clients wish to raise with the mediator but do not want to share with the other party, as, for example, their desire to settle because they are not comfortable about going to court. It could concern your clients' desire to determine what the chances are for a settlement.

It is also an opportunity for you and your clients to find out whether your clients should or should not share certain information with the other party, as, for example, personal or corporate information. It also provides the mediator with the possibility of giving you information, on a confidential basis, which could be useful to you and your client.

The caucus also gives you the possibility of asking the mediator for an opinion of a given proposal made by the other party, to settle the conflict. Some mediators are reluctant to give their opinion on such a question. However, other mediators may provide you and your client with their thoughts on the matter and encourage or discourage your clients to accept the other party's proposal. They may also point to pertinent caselaw to guide you.

Irrespective of the subject matter, you should be open and confide in the mediator. A caucus allows for an exchange of information that will allow the mediator to better help bring about a settlement and will help you to move forward in your negotiations.

### t) To Provide the Mediator with Your Clients' Bottom Line

Finally, a caucus allows you to advise to the mediator as to your clients' bottom line. As already indicated, you can be open with this information since the caucus is a confidential meeting within the mediation.

The proposal that you give to the mediator may be your clients' final offer. If it is not accepted, your clients will either institute a lawsuit or, if a lawsuit has already been filed, they will continue their proceedings and go to trial.

While you may conclude that your clients will not offer more (if they are the defendants) or accept less (if they are the plaintiffs), there is often just a small amount separating the parties' positions, such that a minor change in each party's so-called *final position* will result in an agreement.

The parties set out their initial position at the beginning of a mediation session. However, as the mediation progresses, and as more information is exchanged, the parties generally re-evaluate how realistic their stand is. They almost always move from an initial position.

Consequently, as the mediation evolves, you will see what amount of movement there is in the other party's position. At some point, there will be less and less give and take, until one party or the other becomes unyielding. It may be your clients who decide they will not offer more or that they will not accept less than a certain amount, or it may be the other party. The same applies to any non-monetary solution.

The time to tell the mediator what constitutes your clients' bottom line is after a series of fruitful negotiations that gradually slow, so that there is truly little movement in the proposals.

It is preferable to discuss this matter in caucus with the mediator, who will be in the privileged position of determining whether the parties' positions are close to each other and whether it will take little to close the gap or whether some alternatives or some modalities with respect to the payment should be considered in order to reach a settlement.

### 15) Caucus Versus Plenary Sessions

Different mediators work differently in terms of whether they use the plenary session or caucuses. To a certain extent, the nature of the conflict also determines how the mediation will proceed.

Mediation in separation, divorce, or other family conflicts are usually dealt with in plenary sessions, particularly when the issues concern the couple's children. The parties remain together in their negotiations and discussions with the mediator. There is an attempt to find a solution for each aspect of the conflict in a collaborative manner. It is important for both parties to communicate directly with each other to understand the other party's perspective and feelings in searching for appropriate solutions. This way of proceeding better ensures that the interests of the children are considered by both parents together.

Some mediators use only the plenary session, irrespective of the nature of the conflict. It ensures that the parties are aware of each other's interests. The plenary session also ensures better collaboration in seeking a resolution of conflict than when the parties deal with the issues independently from each other.

In other types of disputes, typically where the hostility is extremely high, or in cases of an extreme power imbalance, the mediation will more often take place by caucusing. The parties remain in separate rooms, with the mediator going back and forth between the parties and their lawyers, conveying offers, counteroffers, and the parties' reactions from one to another. This is known as *shuttle diplomacy*. The same process can take place virtually, with the mediator using breakout rooms to speak to each party separately, without the other party hearing or seeing what takes place.

The most usual method used in mediations involves a combination of plenary sessions and caucuses. The parties begin in the plenary session and break out into a caucus, as the need arises. There may be one or several caucuses. When mediators hold a caucus with one of the parties, they will usually caucus with the other party as well, to preserve their position and appearance of neutrality, even if there is no need to meet with the other party and counsel at that time.

After each caucus, the mediator may ask the parties to return to the plenary session to discuss the latest proposals, to confirm any agreements reached on some of the issues, to encourage movement, or to brainstorm with both parties present. The mediator may also continue to caucus with the parties if this way of proceeding proves to be more effective.

### 16) Impasses

An impasse is a deadlock in the negotiations. Put differently, it is a position that is taken and from that stand no further progress takes place. It is not uncommon for an impasse to occur at some point during the mediation.

It is important to distinguish between a negotiating tactic on the part of one of the parties and a true impasse.

Sometimes parties will indicate that the proposal they have just made is their last or they will simply say that they are not prepared to offer more (if they are the defendants) or they are not prepared to accept the amount offered (if they are the plaintiffs). The opposing party and counsel then say they are not altering their position. These statements may, in fact, reflect the parties' final proposals, or they may simply be a step in the process of trying to reach a pre-established goal on the part of one or the other party.

When an actual impasse arises, there are means of dealing with it. This is generally the job of the mediator. The various tools used by mediators to break the deadlock are explained here.

Mediators, in trying to overcome the impasse, may:

- suggest a caucus,
- keep silent when the others have stopped talking,
- raise possible propositions,
- identify the interests of the parties,
- contact a third party,
- take a break in the mediation,
- ask the parties to consider another issue on the table,
- ask the parties to brainstorm or think outside the box to propose an alternative solution, such as an offer of goods or services,
- use role playing and ask the parties to articulate the position of the opposing party,
- use humour,
- ask to meet with the lawyers without their clients,
- ask to meet with the clients without their lawyers,
- ask questions regarding the basis of their positions,
- point out the progress already made, using a flip chart or a blackboard,
- discuss the risks of not settling,
- talk about the best- and worst-case scenarios if the parties go to trial, or
- indicate that the parties are not far apart, pointing out that it is not reasonable to go to court when the difference between them is so small.

Most often, mediators will ask each party and their lawyer to meet with them in a caucus where they can raise various issues, such as the weaknesses of each party's position, the lack of reasonableness of an adopted position, the delay in obtaining a judgment, the cost of litigation, the risks involved in going to trial, and so on.

Mediators can also ask questions to have the lawyers reconsider their positions by pointing to the current status of the caselaw on the issue in question, the impact of the disputed facts in their case, the alternatives to negotiating a settlement, and other points that will lead each party to re-evaluate their respective stands.

Other points can be raised, such as asking whether a non-monetary solution could be envisaged as a solution or whether there is a possibility for the parties to re-establish their relations. Mediators can also try to close the gap by encouraging one of the parties to ante up the amount offered or by asking a party to make a concession in response to a concession made by the other party.

Another possibility is to ask the plaintiffs to write down the most they think the defendants will offer and ask the defendants to write down what they think is the least amount the plaintiffs will accept. Often the two amounts, once revealed, are remarkably close to each other and are very realistic as a possible solution.

In the privacy of the caucus, mediators may even put forward their opinion as to the potential outcome of the case in court, after having won over the trust of everyone involved.

When all else has failed, mediators may provide positive statements and make a plea for compromise and for the resolution of the conflict.

Finally, mediators may suggest a possible solution. This does not pose a problem if, rather than telling the parties what proposal they should accept, mediators present a possible proposal in such a way that will bring about a discussion between the parties. For example, the mediator could ask: *Would X and Y be a possibility that you could envisage to resolve the conflict, and if so, how could it be implemented?*

Although mediators will deal with a deadlock in the negotiations, nothing prevents you, as counsel, from actively participating in the mediation and using the same methods listed above as a means to help unblock an impasse. The following are some of the methods you can use, even when the mediator has not suggested them.

### a) Ask for a Caucus

An impasse can occur because of a lack of sufficient information. It may be helpful to try to obtain the facts that you need from your clients or, alternatively, to ask the mediator whether any missing facts can be obtained from the other party or their counsel.

Meeting the mediator in a caucus with your clients is always a means of moving forward. The caucus provides the possibility of obtaining information from the mediator which can help you determine whether your clients should change their approach or how they should modify their proposals.

In the classic approach to mediation, as already indicated, mediators do not provide their opinion on the case. In interest-based mediations, the legal rights of the parties are not important. However, some mediators will provide their view on the potential outcome of a case if they are asked for their opinion in a caucus.

Although most mediators are not prepared to express their views on the outcome of a case in the plenary session, they may nevertheless be ready to identify the weaknesses of your clients' case in a caucus. This will allow you to discuss this issue with your clients and potentially re-evaluate your position.

If, on the other hand, the mediator believes that you have several strong points, you can use the caucus to request that the mediator transmit this information to the other party, with the hope that it will serve to induce the opposite party to modify their position.

In short, such discussions can be constructive in dealing with an impasse.

### b) Contact a Third Party

Occasionally, an impasse results because further information is needed from a third party in order to resolve a problem. There may be financial considerations to contemplate in reaching a solution on the damages payable, which can be resolved with the input of an accountant or a tax specialist. An architect or an engineer might be instrumental in resolving a conflict concerning a problem related to a building's structure. In a construction conflict, a contractor can provide a dollar figure regarding the cost to repair or make suggestions about different methods that can be used to rectify the problem raised. In a family conflict, a psychologist or social worker could contribute positively to the problem in question.

An independent person can provide information or an opinion on some aspect of the issue that has created the blockage, such that it will overcome the impasse.

### c) Raise Possible Propositions

You may also consider posing a few questions to lead the opposing party to consider other options or reconsider their position. Some possible questions, including a number listed in Section 7, are the following:

- What would happen if the agreement included…
- Can you envisage the possibility of X as an option?
- Would you be willing to consider X, if we accepted Y?
- If we took X off the table, would you remove Y from your demands?
- Would you agree to obtain more information on this option?
- Would you agree to consult an engineer (architect, etc.) for their opinion on the issue?
- Do we understand that you would consider X as a substitute for our present proposal?
- You indicated that your position on X was not final. Are we correct in our understanding of your position?
- Is this item essential for you and are there other important items that we could consider?
- Can you put yourself in our shoes? What would you do to resolve this aspect of the conflict?
- Would X work for both parties?
- What would you give up to obtain what you are seeking?
- What item on your list would you not give up?
- What do you object to about our proposal?
- What will take place if we do not settle?

By posing questions in this way, you and your clients are asking for the opposing party's help in finding a solution. You are more likely to obtain a positive response if you ask whether a certain idea could be acceptable first, before making a formal proposal.

### d) Ask Questions

Often when parties are deadlocked in their positions, neither party thinks of asking appropriate questions that may require the other party to explain their stand. Consider asking the following questions to gain information on certain aspects of the claim:

- What is the basis of your position?
- What standards have you used?
- How did you decide on that amount?
- What is the applicable market value?
- What do you consider to be a fair price?
- What arrangement (in family matters) do you think is fair for both parties?
- Would you allow an expert to evaluate the problem and provide us with a fair price?
- Have you considered prices that are competitive?
- Have you considered precedents on this issue?

The purpose of asking such questions is to move away from positional bargaining and have the opposing party and their lawyer consider standards that can be used to break an impasse. There is a better chance of reaching an agreement that both parties can accept when they believe the outcome is fair or based on some kind of rational standard.

### e) Meet Privately with the Other Lawyer

When the parties will not yield and a stalemate occurs, it may be useful to approach the opposing party's lawyer and propose a meeting between the two of you.

When there is a real desire for a settlement, but the parties are unable to alter their positions, it is often the lawyers who, with some creativity, can bring about a rapprochement.

It is sometimes fruitful for the two attorneys to discuss what they consider to be a reasonable solution for both parties. Then, it becomes a matter of determining what it will take to have one or the other, or both parties, move from the position they have adopted.

The two lawyers can brainstorm and try to find the means of convincing either their own clients or both parties to modify their last proposal. The possibilities for doing so include:

- Suggesting another solution that has not been discussed.
- Suggesting that one or the other review the legal aspects of the case in private with their clients and emphasize a weakness in their position.
- In cases where a party has an unrealistic view of the case, recommending that the party's lawyer discuss with their clients the potential outcome of their case at trial and try to convince their clients to accept a more objective perspective.
- Advising the clients of the decisions that the courts have rendered in similar cases.
- Reiterating the risk of going to trial where they cannot be certain that the judgment that will be rendered will be in their favour.

Although the suggestions listed above for dealing with a stalemate do not guarantee that the parties will move forward in their negotiations, if both lawyers collaborate, they can nevertheless be instrumental in inducing their clients to settle.

#### f) Have the Parties Meet Alone

While lawyers are present to help their clients come to an agreement, there are times where, rather than helping their clients, lawyers are divisive and present roadblocks to any possible settlement.

It is not common to have the parties meet on their own, without the presence of their lawyers and the mediator. However, in cases where the lawyer representing the other party continually negates any proposal that is presented, it is in your clients' interest to continue discussions without the negative impact of the opposing lawyer.

Mediators are reluctant to ask that the parties meet on their own. They do not want to interfere in a client-lawyer relationship.

However, nothing prevents you from asking the opposing lawyer to consider the possibility for the parties speak to each other privately. The opposing lawyer may not agree, because of concerns that the client will not be counselled during the discussions with respect to any potential proposals made. But if the opposing lawyer accepts your suggestion, and if the parties are willing to meet with each other, there is a chance that they will be able to find a solution on their own.

There are occasions when the parties have known each other for a lengthy period, in a friendship, or in a business or an employment relationship. In such long-standing relations with each other, the parties truly know what happened and are often able to speak frankly to each other, in the absence of anyone monitoring their discussions. It is not uncommon for them to figure out what kind of outcome will work for both and what will allow them to put an end to their conflict.

The instances where the discussions between the parties on their own can be successful include not only those when the blockage stems from an unreasonable position on the part of one of the lawyers, or the existence of a long-standing relationship between the parties, but also when the parties have a common culture and language that is different from their lawyers and the mediator. In such cases, the parties are often more comfortable communicating with each other in their own language.

Obviously, these scenarios are only possible if the parties can deal with each other without hostility or aggression.

### g) Take a Break

After some time, the parties may become tired, frustrated, and intransigent. They may even declare that they are leaving because there is no chance of a settlement. This is an opportune time to take a break from the mediation session. Whether you go for coffee, take a walk outside or simply move into another room, this is a time to reflect before giving up on the process.

Remind your clients that the goal is not to win their case or persuade the opposing party that they are right. Talk to your clients about the possibility of a final compromise, about what type of settlement they can live with, and about the risks involved if they do not settle, while never forgetting that the final decision belongs to your clients. Encourage them to return to the plenary session with a positive attitude and make a final attempt to resolve the conflict.

#### h) Discuss the Risk of Going to Court

You should raise the risk of going to trial, pointing to your opponent's weaknesses and their best and worst outcomes if they go to court. Remind the opposing party that no matter how solid a case they think they have, there is always a risk that their position will not be upheld by a judge.

Raise the issue of the costs involved. Ask the opposing party and counsel whether they have evaluated the cost of a trial, which not only includes a client's legal fees but also the probable business losses because of the time spent in court. In addition, remind them to consider the stress and emotional cost of a trial as well. If, after negotiations have taken place for some time and the parties are only apart by a small amount of money, you could consider telling the opposing party that it is unreasonable to go to court, given the small gap between the parties.

### 17) Alternate and Creative Proposals — Thinking Outside the Box

When the parties are unyielding with respect to a monetary proposal, with each party maintaining the same proposal and neither modifying their position, it is a good idea to ask whether there are alternate solutions that can be proposed, irrespective of whether your clients are the ones claiming a sum of money or whether they are the ones from whom money is sought.

When reflecting on alternate solutions, look for items that are of a low cost for the party who will be paying and of high benefit for the party who will be the recipient. This type of proposal will satisfy both parties.

Some of the questions that you should consider are the following:

- Are there other issues to be resolved in the conflict?
- Can the amount of money to be paid be set aside so that the parties deal with another matter and return to the monetary discussions a little later?
- Can the monetary compensation be combined with another benefit that would bring about a settlement?
- Would it be possible to provide a service rather than a sum of money, or would it be possible to include the provision of a service as part of the settlement?

Most parties think only of the amount of monetary compensation to be paid. They fail to think outside the box. Creative thinking is often greatly beneficial. The following is a non-exhaustive list of some of the positive outcomes from mediations.

In construction conflicts:

- An undertaking by a contractor to have work redone with different employees or different materials, rather than paying any money.
- Obtaining an independent evaluation of the damages or work done to determine the amount payable.
- Evaluating the depreciation of the property.
- Determining the awards courts have granted in similar cases.

In conflicts regarding service contracts:

- Accountants, architects, engineers, psychologists, and other professionals agreeing to provide services for the other party, after determining what amount of time would correspond to the monetary compensation payable.
- Travel agents agreeing to provide a trip to another destination, following a complaint alleging terrible accommodations at an all-inclusive resort.
- Airlines agreeing to provide a ticket together with an upgrade, which can be used at a future date, following a flight cancellation that ruined vacations plans.

In dismissal cases:

- A company agreeing to provide the employee with equipment or access to equipment needed to start a business.
- Providing resources for the employee to set up a business.
- A letter of recommendation for the employee that is drafted jointly by both parties.
- Providing for outsourcing services.
- Providing services to upgrade the employee' skills.
- Providing retraining.
- An apology.

In conflicts regarding leased premises:

- Offering to repaint the premises.
- Agreeing to provide additional services or equipment.
- Effecting necessary and outstanding repairs.
- Renegotiating the terms and conditions of the lease.

Examples in other matters:

- Agreeing to submit the question to an expert for an opinion.
- Submitting the issue to an evaluator to determine the value of a property or an object.
- Using objective standards, such as the market value, court decisions, legal standards, professional standards, scientific criteria, building norms, and so on.

These and other types of proposals can bring about an agreement but are often not considered by the parties when their focus is only on a dollar figure. Such non-monetary proposals can be offered either alone or in addition to monetary compensation. They are often a means to bring the conflict to an end.

When only a monetary solution is envisaged, modalities can nevertheless be considered. These can include the amount of interest payable, making payments in instalments, allowing for more flexibility in the timing and frequency of the instalment payments, and so on.

### 18) Persuading the Other Party

One means of influencing the other party is having what is called a Best Alternative to a Negotiated Agreement (BATNA). This involves informing the other party that your clients have a better alternative to a settlement. This can be an effective means of persuasion to obtain more from the other party (if your clients are the plaintiffs) or to offer less (if your clients are the defendants), provided that the opposing party believes that what you have said is true.

In cases where there are common interests, do not be reluctant to talk about them. For example, your clients could remind the other party that they are both running businesses and it will be a costly proposition for both of them to spend days in a courtroom, or your clients can refer to both parties' desire to keep the case confidential, and so on. Try appealing to their commitment to reach an agreement and ask what they think can finalize the deal.

The relationship between the parties can impact the ease of their ability to reach an agreement. There is more likelihood of influencing the other party when both parties respect and trust each other.

Good communication skills are also important as a means of persuasion. For example, having your clients indicate that they have understood the other party's perspective, even if they do not agree, will lead that party to listen more attentively to your clients' interests and needs than if your clients are not paying attention when the opposing party is speaking.

In addition, it is appropriate to refer to established criteria for a settlement in your case and point to other comparable cases as examples, to show the other party that your proposal is fair. Finally, have your clients make a firm offer that will not be available again in the future if it is refused now.

## 19) The Process of Considering Proposals

Each time a proposal is put forward, your clients may want to confer with you to determine whether it is acceptable, or they may feel comfortable responding on their own, particularly if you have already discussed what they are seeking and what are the potential outcomes.

If one of parties puts forward a proposal that may be a possible solution, it usually is discussed further. If, on the other hand, a proposal is not accepted, counteroffers can be made. Further proposals may be presented, followed by more counter proposals. However, if a proposal is entirely unacceptable, you should think about searching for an alternate means of settling, and the same process will take place. This back-and-forth will continue throughout the entire mediation.

How the negotiations play out will also depend on whether both parties present proposals that are reasonable. Each proposal should be considered as a possible suggestion for a solution and not a final one. To be effective, a proposal should be in the realm of what is considered credible. If both parties present reasonable proposals, there is often a likelihood that the acceptable outcome will be somewhere between the two reasonable propositions, although this may not necessarily be the case, particularly when one or the other party has a final amount in mind,

The opposing party often will suggest a figure that is in between the last proposal and your clients' proposal. If the plaintiffs' last proposal was $80,000 and the defendants countered with an offer of $40,000, the defendants may expect that the final result of their negotiations will be $60,000. However, nothing prevents the plaintiffs from asking for $78,000 and then decreasing their demand by $1,000 for each ensuing proposal, if they are aiming for a resolution at $75,000. Similarly, the defendants can act in the same way, increasing their offers minimally, if they are hoping to end with the acceptance of a final proposal of $45,000. Therefore, you should advise your clients to consider each proposal carefully to determine what the next one will be.

During the negotiations, the parties often suggest various options. The mediator may list the proposals on a flip chart or a blackboard for easy reference as well as to show what progress has been made. The parties are encouraged to list as many options as possible, and not to reject any one straight away. When the parties have put several proposals on the table, a process of elimination takes place, until there is an option or options that are acceptable to the parties.

When several issues are involved in a conflict, the mediator will suggest that the parties deal with them one at a time and try to resolve each of them before moving on to the next. When any issue is problematic, it is best left to the end. Usually, when most items are settled, it is easier to come to an agreement on any outstanding issue or issues.

### 20) The Final Offer

It is not uncommon that one or the other party gets to the point where they no longer wish to negotiate any further and state: *This is my final offer; take it or leave it.* Often the proposal is close to the final one, but it is not the very last in the negotiating process. It is important not to give up but try to see if there is any possibility of moving a little closer to reach a compromise.

If the other party indicates that the last proposal is final, and although it is not totally acceptable to your clients, it is close to the outcome they are seeking, you could simply tell the other party that you are remarkably close to reaching an agreement, but you need the other party to sweeten the deal. Sometimes, adding just a little to the so-called final offer (by the defendants) or accepting a little less (by the plaintiffs) can result in a breakthrough.

However, if the other party truly means that the last proposal is the final one and not a tactic, the reality is that if your clients do not accept the proposal, the other party is prepared to end the talks and go to court.

In such a situation, you must discuss, with your clients, whether they can live with this final position or whether they are prepared to face a trial. Alternatively, you may consider making one further proposal, while at the same time pointing out the risks of going to court.

## 21) Evaluating the Options and the Selection

In preparing for the mediation, you have discussed the outcome that your clients are prepared to accept. However, at the mediation, new information and proposals that you had not expected may be presented. It is therefore useful during the negotiations to evaluate what is an acceptable outcome for your clients. Before accepting any offer that will put an end to the conflict, you should review the best-case scenario and the worst-case scenario that you envisage if you go to court. This allows you to better advise your clients as to the benefit of concluding an agreement based on the last proposition(s).

For example, if your clients have sued after purchasing a house with an alleged hidden defect, you should determine the possible outcomes that will result from a judgment. Assume that the repairs have been evaluated at $300,000 and you have instituted a lawsuit, on behalf of your clients, for this amount in damages. In one possible outcome, the court could conclude that the defect was apparent, in which case, your clients will lose their lawsuit entirely. This, of course, is the worst-case scenario.

Alternatively, your clients may only be granted part of the amount sought after the court has taken into consideration the depreciation or the life of one of the items involved (as in the case of a leaking roof which is near the end of its lifespan). Assume that the court concludes that your clients' case has merit, but only grants $260,000 after evaluating the depreciation of the roof. In such a case, your clients would be partially successful.

Finally, your clients may succeed entirely in their claim and be awarded $300,000 by the court.

However, in each of the two latter examples, there are costs involved that must also be factored in, in evaluating how much your clients will potentially get if they go to trial and obtain a judgment in their favour.

Assume that you have estimated the cost of an expert report and the expert's testimony in court to amount to $25,000. You have estimated your fees to come to $75,000 by the end of the trial. If your clients' case were upheld completely, they would obtain at most $200,000 after a trial, rather than $300,000. This sum does not include any court costs or loss of revenue because of your clients' absence from their business, professions, or jobs while they prepare for and attend a trial. This is the best-case scenario if your clients *win* their lawsuit.

In the case where the court takes depreciation into account and awards $260,000, after you deduct the costs of the expert and your fees — amounting to a total of $100,000 — your clients would obtain an amount of $160,000, without even considering court costs and their loss of revenue.

Accordingly, if you conclude that the other party's best proposal in mediation is as good as or better than the best outcome that your clients can obtain from court, after deducting all of their costs, you will be most comfortable advising your clients to accept that offer.

If, on the other hand, you conclude that the other side's proposal does not meet your clients' best interests, you should tell the opposing party that you believe your clients' worst-case scenario at court is still better than what the opposing party is proposing. This may lead your opponent to reconsider and try to find a solution that is positive, not only for your clients but for the opponent as well.

Therefore, in negotiating, your clients should point out the amount of their claim in the lawsuit ($300,000, in the above example), while stating that in the interest of settling they are prepared to compromise. They could say that they would be willing to accept $275,000 to resolve the case (leaving some room to negotiate further in the hope of obtaining $250,000).

As the negotiations proceed with offers and counteroffers, you and your clients should be considering their best-case scenario.

In the example given above, if depreciation is not involved, any amount of $200,000 or more would be acceptable. If you anticipate that the court will consider and apply depreciation in its award, you must reduce this sum accordingly.

Finally, in advising your clients as to their final selection of the options which have been put forward, you must ensure that any solution chosen is one that reconciles with your clients' interests and needs and is satisfactory to them.

One last comment. If the final proposal is not acceptable to your clients and it is clear that the mediation session will end without an agreement, consider the possibility of asking the mediator to keep the file open for a short period of time. As indicated in the final comments of this text, it is not unusual for parties to think about the consequences of their decisions following the mediation and, after serious reflection, decide to compromise further and settle their case.

## F. POWER IMBALANCE

Power refers to the ability to influence situations or outcomes. It can impact the perceptions and behaviour of those affected.[13] Mediation sessions are intended to be fair and carried out in a level playing field. However, it is rare that power between the parties is equal or balanced in a conflict.

Power is a concern in mediation because the outcome is affected by the ability of the parties to negotiate effectively. When there is a difference in power, or a power imbalance, with the result that one party is able to assert their power and dominate the process to the disadvantage of the other party, the mediation process is threatened. In such cases, any agreement that is reached will be unfair and meet only the interests and needs of

---

13 Scottish Community Mediation Centre, "Power Imbalances in Mediation," online: www.scmc.sacro.org.uk/sites/default/files/resource/SCMC_9_PowerImbalancesInMediation.pdf.

the dominant player, to the detriment of the other party.[14] The weaker party may be pressured, intimidated, or coerced to conclude an agreement, ultimately conceding too many elements of their claim or defence. As a result, their consent to an agreement may not be voluntary.

Most think about a power imbalance as consisting of greater financial means and authority. In reality, various types of power imbalances exist. In addition to financial and positional power, many factors influence the power a person has. Power can stem from physical strength, size, force, status, high self-esteem, personal attributes such as attractiveness and charisma, articulateness, intellectual ability, knowledge, education, experience, emotional control, differences in age, class, race, gender, and sexual orientation, as well as religious, moral, political, and cultural factors. It can also result from the ability to reward or sanction another person.[15]

Power is relative. It exists vis-à-vis another person and can vary depending on the situation. Imbalances often occur in conflicts involving an employer and an employee or a landlord and a tenant, and in cases of family affairs involving domestic abuse. When the power differences are significant, mediation is not the appropriate forum to resolve the conflict. This is particularly so in family conflicts where an individual's ability to negotiate without the fear of reprisals is jeopardized by a history of violence. With the exception of extreme cases, most instances of power imbalances can be managed.

It is important for lawyers to recognize a power imbalance and intervene to assist their clients and support them in the process.

---

14 Claire Baylis & Robyn Carroll, "The Nature and Importance of Mechanisms for Addressing Power Differences in Statutory Mediation" (2002) 14 *Bond Law Review* 287 at 291.

15 Emily Holland, "When a Power Imbalance Exists: Identifying a Power Imbalance" *ADR Times* (13 February 2023), online: www.adrtimes.com/when-a-power-imbalance-exists; Anne D. Carey, "How to Mediate Amid a Power Imbalance" *Litigation & ADR Lawyer Monthly Interview Magazine* (28 February 2022), online: www.lawyer-monthly.com/2022/02/how-to-mediate-amid-a-power-imbalance; Felicia Staub, "The Effect of Power in Mediation" *Mediate.com* (17 January 2020), online: https://mediate.com/the-effect-of-power-in-mediation.

Some of the behaviours that a party will show that should alert you to a power imbalance include a reluctance to talk, the inability to assert their position, allowing the opposing party to interrupt the presentation or proposal, withdrawing from participation, and other similar comportment. If you are representing a less powerful party, there are several means of intervening that can be useful. The following are examples of the ways in which a lawyer can intervene.

Encourage your clients to express themselves by asking questions or suggesting that they talk about an item that is important to them. As an example, you could say, *You told me about xxx when we met; please tell the other party about what happened and how you felt.* Encourage your clients to give their opinion about the ideas that the opposing party has proposed by asking them how that proposal would be positive for both the parties. Ensure that the other party does not dominate the discussions. If this occurs, intervene and tell the other party that your clients would like to respond.

If your clients are interrupted by the opposite party, do not hesitate to step in and remind the other party that your clients listened without interrupting them when they spoke, and you expect them to listen when your clients are speaking.

Ask for a caucus if you notice that your clients have become anxious, overly quiet, withdrawn, and/or submissive. This will slow the pace of the negotiations and allow you to provide your clients with appropriate information and support.

Ask the mediator to proceed by means of shuttle mediation so that the parties are not in the same room, explaining to the mediator in a caucus the reason for your request. Ask for a break in the mediation to provide support and encouragement to your clients. Ensure that your clients understand a proposal put forward by the opposite party by addressing any potential misunderstandings that may arise. Summarize, paraphrase, and explain what the other party has suggested as a possible solution to the conflict. Make sure that the final proposal on the table is fair to your clients and meets their needs and interests.

If an agreement has been reached, ask for a delay before your clients sign it to make sure that they are comfortable with the content of the settlement agreement and that they have not concluded an agreement out of fear or intimidation. Ensure that your clients fully understand the outcome and consequences of a proposed agreement before they agree to accept it. If, despite your best efforts, your clients feel overwhelmed and dominated by the opposing party, and you believe they are at a clear disadvantage in the process, you can leave the mediation session with your clients.

Lawyers should be aware and vigilant of power imbalances even when they represent clients who are more powerful and assertive than the opposing party. If your clients are overly domineering, there is the risk that the opposing party will feel so threatened that they leave the mediation session. It is also possible that if they do remain at the mediation, they will refuse to conclude an agreement. Another risk is that if the weaker party reaches an agreement with your clients but feels that they were pressured into signing the settlement, that party will refuse to respect the settlement.

Accordingly, it is important that you counsel your clients to listen to the opposing party's ideas and viewpoints and avoid acting in an aggressive, intimidating, or coercive manner. Remind your clients of the potential consequences that may ensue if they behave in this way.

Finally, before the mediation session, ask your clients about the attributes of the other party and try to determine beforehand the extent to which the power between the parties will be unequal. If you foresee the probability of a power imbalance at the mediation, discuss with your clients the various strategies (listed above) that can be adopted at the mediation session to deal with the power differences. This will allow your clients to feel more secure once they are at the mediation.

## G. PROFESSONAL RESPONSIBILITY

Many standards have been adopted to address ethical standards for mediators, as, for example, the obligation of impartiality and neutrality, maintaining confidentiality, avoidance of conflicts of interest or claims of having particular expertise when none exists, and so on. The representation of clients in mediation places ethical and professional obligations on lawyers as well. However, there is far less guidance concerning the standards for lawyers who represent their clients in mediation than for lawyers in other situations.[16]

Bar associations across Canada have established a code of ethics governing the practice of law. However, in contrast to the United States, where bar associations have produced ethical guidelines for lawyers representing clients in settlement negotiations, it appears that Canadian institutions have not found it necessary to adopt such guidelines for lawyers in Canada.[17] There is nevertheless conduct that should be respected by lawyers who represent their clients in mediations, based not only on a lawyer's code of professional conduct but also on moral considerations.

It is not unusual for lawyers who accompany their clients in a mediation session to deliberately derail the process. They may try to control the process or attempt to litigate. They may dissuade a client from accepting a reasonable offer in the hope of obtaining greater compensation from a trial.[18] Alternatively, they may bully clients to settle their conflict in mediation, against their clients' wishes, rather than go to court or arbitration.[19] They may come to the mediation unprepared or, more often, not having prepared their clients sufficiently to be able to present their version of the facts and to negotiate properly.

---

16 John A. Sherill, "Ethics for Lawyers Representing Clients in Mediations" *American Journal of Mediation* (2012), online: americanjournalofmediation.com/docs/JOHN%20SHERRILL%20-Ethics%20for%20Lawyers%20Representing%20Clients%20in%20Mediation.pdf.

17 Collin P. Stevenson, "Ethics and Settlement: Let Right Prevail" Stevenson Whelton Barristers (17 November 2011), online: www.swlawyers.ca/wp-content/uploads/2019/06/Ethics-and-Settlement_-_Let-Right-Prevail_-_Colin-Stevenson.pdf.

18 Ani Comfort Chinyere, "Mediation Ethics and Analogous Issues" *Legalpedia Online* (2 October 2020), online: https://legalpediaonline.com/mediation-ethics.

19 Deanne Sower, Mediation: "A Warning Not to Bully a Client into Settlement" *Slaw: Canada's Online Legal Magazine* (18 September 2020), online: www.slaw.ca/2020/09/18/mediation-a-warning-not-to-bully-a-client-into-settlement.

While all lawyers must respect their bar association's governing code of conduct and, in so doing, must act in the best interests of their clients, there are certain considerations that are specifically applicable to mediations.

Lawyers must inform their clients of the various means of settling conflicts. It is their duty to provide the necessary information so that their clients can make an informed decision. If mediation is the appropriate method to resolve the conflict, it is then up to the clients to decide whether they want to participate in a mediation session. It is also the clients' decision as to the objective sought, which can range from obtaining a sum of money to re-establishing a business or a personal relationship.

Rather than representing a client in a zealous manner, as is standard in an adversarial situation where the objective is to win, it is more appropriate in mediation to act in a collaborative way.[20] Zealous representation or acting in an obstructive way is not consistent with the objectives of dispute resolution.

Lawyers must respect the requirement of confidentiality in the mediation process, irrespective of whether they signed a protocol to this effect. Lawyers must understand their clients' perspectives and ensure during the entire mediation process that their clients' needs are being met.

Lawyers must be candid with their clients by providing information and advice during the mediation session. They must advise their clients as to how the mediation is progressing and give them an honest assessment of their case, which may involve unwelcome facts, a re-evaluation, or alternatives regarding the clients' position, even when a modified approach is not what their clients wish to hear.

Lawyers should discuss with their clients not only all legal aspects involved in their case but also other relevant considerations, such as the moral, financial, and social factors that may be

20 See Sherill, above note 16.

relevant to the situation,[21] as well as the emotional cost of pursuing a case given the delays, stress, and expense related to a trial. Accordingly, lawyers must encourage their clients to examine not only a monetary settlement but also other reasonable alternatives.

In cases where a lawyer believes that a better outcome can be obtained in court, the lawyer must nevertheless consider what is best for their clients, taking into consideration their clients' ability to withstand the delays, pressure, and the costs of a trial. After providing the requisite advice on the last available option, and discussing it with clients, the decision as to whether or not to accept a settlement offer is ultimately up to the clients. Once the client decides the matter, the lawyer must accept the clients' decision.

When clients wish to accept a final proposal, it is the role of the lawyer to review the proposed agreement and to ensure that it meets the clients' best interests, goals, and objectives. It is also important that lawyers review all the clauses to ensure that there are no ambiguities. Conversely, when clients do not want to accept the terms proposed by the opposite party, lawyers should not unduly urge them to settle.

Lawyers have an obligation to be honest in exercising their mandates. In mediation, however, it is not unusual for lawyers to engage in deceptive behaviour by providing incomplete or misleading information, which is sometimes referred to as *puffing* or *hyperbole*.[22] An example can include statements denying that your clients will settle for a certain sum of money even though they authorized you to pay that amount or insisting that your clients' bottom line is a certain amount when in fact they will settle for less. Estimates of price or a party's intentions also fall into this category.

---

21 *Ibid*; see also Lawrence H. Hoover, Jr., "Advocacy in Mediation: Ethics" presented in CLE programs "Advocacy in Mediation" (1999), online: www.mccammongroup.com/articles/advocacy-mediation-ethics.

22 Marcy Einhorn, "An Overview of the New York Rules of Professional Conduct in the Context of Mediation" (17 November 2017), online: https://mediate.com/an-overview-of-the-new-york-rules-of-professional-conduct-in-the-context-of-mediation; Stevenson, above note 17 at 5.

Such cases illustrate an attempt to have clients pay less, if the clients are the defendants, or obtain more, if the clients are the plaintiffs. Puffing is recognized as part of the negotiation process and does not constitute misrepresentation, provided that the allegations do not materially misstate the facts.

Ethical experts have expressed differing opinions on what standards of truthfulness apply in mediations.[23] However, while there is not a complete consensus on this question, being candid and forthright will more likely result in a positive result and achieve the objectives of your clients.

Finally, although the goal in selecting mediation as a dispute resolution method is a negotiated settlement with the opposite party, there are nevertheless situations where it is preferable to have your clients leave the mediation and turn to the courts to deal with the conflict. Such situations include cases where your clients are subjected to bullying, aggression, a significant power imbalance, or a fishing expedition by the opposing lawyer or party, in the absence of appropriate intervention by the mediator.

23 Stevenson, above note 17.

*chapter six*

# Conclusions

Initially, when I began mediating, if an agreement was reached, the lawyers would prepare a list of the items that were settled by their clients and then draft the final provisions later, in their respective offices. This was not an ideal solution, because sometimes once the mediation was over, and the lawyers set out the terms of the agreement, disagreements occurred over what exactly the parties had agreed upon.

As computers became more prevalent, lawyers were able to draft the terms and conditions agreed upon at the end of the mediation process, such that the parties could read the contents of their agreement together and their lawyers could provide them with any necessary explanations. As a result, the parties could proceed to sign the completed document that day.

Some time later, I noted that the lawyers would often come to the mediation session not only with their computer, but with a draft agreement as well. The draft was subject to whatever final agreements the parties reached, and the terms and conditions could be modified as needed.

There are numerous items that must be considered and included in a settlement agreement to ensure that there is no subsequent ambiguity. Ensuring that the agreement, when drafted, contains clear language and covers all the possibilities that may arise is most important. These details are necessary to avoid conflict in the future regarding what was decided at the mediation.

In the mediation sessions that I presided over, I was always pleased when the lawyers took out a draft agreement from their briefcases at the beginning of the meeting. This meant that not only was there a will on the part of their clients to settle, but there was also optimism on the part of both the lawyers and their clients that an agreement would be reached. In addition, if the parties did settle, then the parties and their lawyers had copies of a potential settlement, and together they could make whatever changes that were needed.

The details regarding the possible outcomes of a mediation session and the content of settlement agreements are set out in this chapter.

❊ ❊ ❊ ❊ ❊

There are three possible outcomes to a mediation: (1) the entire conflict is settled, and if a lawsuit has already been instituted, it will be discontinued; (2) only part of the conflict has been settled, in which case a partial agreement can be drafted; and (3) the case does not settle.

## A. AN AGREEMENT IS REACHED

Once the parties have come to an agreement on the proposal or proposals that will put an end to their conflict, the settlement agreement should be drafted, reviewed, finalized, and signed before the parties leave the mediation session. This is preferable to verbally reaching a settlement and then preparing the actual written agreement subsequently. There are, however, situations where the parties prefer that the final version be drafted and signed later. This may be the case where the parties have reached an agreement in principle but require verification or information on some aspect of the agreement, where consultation with a third party is needed, as, for example, an accountant, or in other situations of a similar nature.

If a settlement agreement is not drafted at the end of the mediation session, at the very least, the proposals and conditions that the parties have agreed to should be listed and initialled by the parties. This will confirm their consent to the agreement that will be prepared later. It also ensures that the final version to be drafted contains all the agreed upon elements. If not, endless discussions can ensue regarding the actual content of the settlement. In extreme cases, the agreement can even unravel. Similarly, it is important that this document contain sufficient detail so that there will be no controversy when the final agreement is to be signed. As well, it is a good idea to specify the need for delay in presenting the settlement agreement to the parties for signature.

In most instances, mediators do not draft the settlement agreement. They do not even participate in preparing it. Generally, the settlement agreement is drafted by the lawyers of both parties. At times, one of the lawyers writes the agreement and the other lawyer reviews the draft. Either lawyer may insist that the language be modified if it does not reflect the intent of the parties.

When preparing a draft settlement agreement, make sure that all the claims are covered. Whether or not you prepare the agreement, you should, at the very least, make a list of all the clauses that are important to your clients, as, for example, whether there will be a single payment or multiple payments, the number of payments if more than one is involved, the amount of each one, whether an alternate form of compensation is foreseen, and so on.

Another possibility in settling conflict in family matters consists of an agreement that will subsequently be presented to the court and incorporated into a consent judgment.

As already indicated, it is important to remind your clients at the end of the mediation session that all discussions and documents exchanged are confidential, irrespective of whether or not the parties reached an agreement. A breach of confidentiality can have serious consequences.

## 1) The Content of a Settlement Agreement

It is important to sufficiently indicate all the terms and conditions of the settlement,[1] including the modalities of putting it into effect and the sanctions involved, if violated. Such detail is necessary to ensure that both parties have the same understanding of what their agreement entails.

Avoid the use of legal terminology. It is important to write the agreement in clear, plain language that is readily comprehensible to the parties, not only to the lawyers. The terms should be specific, clear, and complete.

You should review all aspects of the final settlement with your clients and make sure that they fully understand what has been accepted. Ensure that there are no ambiguities that could create problems in terms of its application.

Some clauses of the agreement are specific to the settlement reached, as for example the sum of money to be paid or the service to be rendered. Other clauses are standard, irrespective of the nature of the settlement. Such clauses include the absence of liability on the part of either party, the confidentiality of the agreement, and the applicable jurisdiction.

## 2) The Parties to the Settlement Agreement

The parties to the settlement agreement must be identified. While they are usually the parties to a lawsuit, they may, in the case of corporations, include the parent or holding companies, subsidiaries, or affiliates. Ensure that all parties bound by the settlement agreement are listed.

---

1 The content of an agreement as listed in this text is compiled from a variety of settlement agreements in mediations over which the author presided, as well as from a checklist by James M. Wagstaffe, "Drafting a Settlement Agreement Checklist (Federal)" *LexisNexis Insights* (3 November 2018), online: https://www.lexisnexis.com/community/insights/legal/practical-guidance-journal/b/pa/posts/drafting-a-settlement-agreement-checklist-federal-1520045041.

### 3) The Preamble or the Recitals

The preamble or the recitals, which appear at the beginning of the settlement agreement, may contain a brief description of the conflict or the plaintiffs' claim, as set out in the lawsuit. It may also contain the execution date of the agreement, although some prefer that the date appear at the end, and it may contain a clause stating that the parties concluded the settlement agreement freely and voluntarily.

### 4) No Admission of Liability

Settlement agreements typically include a clause, either in the preamble/recitals or in the main body of the agreement, indicating that the parties wish to resolve their conflict without any admission of liability, wrongdoing, or obligation on the part of the defendants (or on the part of either party) with respect to their conflict or lawsuit. It is also usual for the parties to state that they wish to terminate their lawsuit and/or avoid any subsequent litigation.

### 5) The Compensation or Consideration That Is Provided

The settlement agreement should clearly indicate the consideration that is to be provided to settle the conflict and any terms related to the performance, whether an amount of money is involved, or another means is foreseen.

#### a) The Payment of a Sum of Money

If the settlement agreement entails a sum of money, indicate who will be paying, to whom the money will be paid, and the amount of money payable. It may also be wise to specify the currency, whether in Canadian dollars, US dollars, or the currency of another country.

Another clause should state whether the payment will be made in one lump sum or whether it will be paid in instalments. If only one payment is to be made, specify the date on which payment must be made. If the payment is to be made in instalments, specify the dates on which the money is payable and how much will be paid in each instalment.

Determine whether the settlement agreement involves the payment of interest on the principal sum, and if so, specify what is the amount of interest that the parties have agreed upon. Indicate whether legal fees or any other costs are to be covered by the agreement.

The settlement agreement should also consider the possibility that the payments will not be made on time. Decide in advance how this situation will be handled, such as how interest will be calculated. You may also wish to add an additional penalty for defaulting.

Other considerations involve determining *how* the funds will be paid. Will the payment be made by means of a cheque, a money order, an e-transfer, or cash? Will the payment be made directly to the plaintiffs, or will it be paid to their lawyer in trust?

It is also important to note where the payment is to be made. If the payment is to be paid directly to the plaintiffs, will it be at the plaintiffs' personal address, business address, or will it be transferred directly to the plaintiffs' bank account? If the payment is to be paid through the intermediary of their lawyer, include the lawyer's address as well as the name of the law firm.

Other factors to consider are the potential tax consequences of the payment. Is it considered as salary in the case of a dismissed employee, with deductions to be made at source, or are the damages qualified as moral damages? Can any part of the amount to be paid to an employee who was dismissed be placed in a registered retirement savings account? Are there taxes that will be payable on the funds received and, if so, what is the amount to be paid?

### b) Provision of a Service

If the settlement agreement involves an alternate means of payment, it is important to indicate elements that should be specified.

For example, if a service is to be provided as a means of settlement, or as part of the settlement, indicate the nature of the service and who will be providing the service. Also specify when the service will be provided and, if it occurs on more than one occasion, the dates on which it will be provided. In cases where a third party is involved, the nature and details of the involvement must be stipulated, as well as the coordinates of that party.

### c) Provision of Goods

The settlement may involve providing goods to the opposing party, rather than a sum of money. If goods are to be provided, a complete description of the goods is needed, as well as the name and coordinates of the supplier or vendor. The agreement must also indicate the date or dates on which the goods will be provided.

Other considerations involve whether a warranty is required for the goods in question and, if so, what the warranty covers and how long the warranty will apply. If equipment or machinery is involved, the agreement may also foresee whether replacement parts will be available and for what duration.

### d) Other Means of Reaching an Agreement

Other means of settling include the reinstatement of a dismissed employee, a letter of recommendation, an apology, and so on.

If the employee's reinstatement is foreseen, the modalities must be specified, including such aspects as when it will take place, what seniority it will entail, and remuneration, if any.

If a letter of recommendation is involved, as in the case of a dismissal, the content of the letter must be drafted, and it should be approved by the defendants. Accordingly, the settlement agreement must specify who will be drafting the letter of recommendation and what it will contain. There should also be a mention as to whether the recipients have any input into the contents of the letter.

Similar considerations apply if an apology is involved. The content of the apology must be determined and drafted after its approval by the opposing party.

In a family law conflict involving the custody of children and visiting rights, the various possibilities of a settlement include whether or not custody is shared. The clauses regarding visiting rights must include details as to the periods of time they take place, the location, the duration, holidays, vacations, and so on.

Appropriate language must be considered for any other methods used in the settlement, whether such means are used alone or in conjunction with the payment of money.

### 6) The Binding Effect of the Settlement Agreement

The settlement agreement generally states that it is binding on the parties to the agreement, on their successors, their assignees, and on their legal representatives, if they sign the agreement.

### 7) Confidentiality

It is important to include a clause regarding confidentiality, namely a statement that the settlement agreement and its contents are confidential and that the parties undertake not to reveal or remit the settlement agreement or its contents to any third party, except if required to do so by law, and except for the purpose of obtaining financial and/or legal advice.

Alternatively, the settlement agreement can stipulate that specific clauses, such as those dealing with the amount of compensation to be paid, be kept confidential, rather than stipulating that the entire agreement is confidential. Provision may be made to indicate the penalty that is applicable if the confidentiality of the settlement agreement is not respected.

Also consider the possibility of including a provision that provides for the parties' response, if questioned about the settlement, which may simply state that the parties have settled all issues between them, in a satisfactory manner, and that they will terminate their lawsuit.

### 8) Governing Law and Jurisdiction

The agreement stipulates the law that will govern the settlement as well as the court or tribunal that will have jurisdiction in respect of any proceeding, in connection with the settlement agreement.

### 9) Release

The agreement usually contains a release clause to cover any conflicts that may arise in the future over the same claims as those settled in the agreement. A general release covers all existing claims and claims that can arise in the future, whether or not they are known, that the releasing party had, has, or may have in the future against the opposing party relating directly or indirectly to the subject matter of the settlement. The release should be drafted so that it is binding on successors and representatives.

### 10) Sanctions

You may wish to consider whether any sanctions will apply if either party fails to respect their agreement, such as a financial penalty. If so, specify the nature of the sanctions.

### 11) Advising the Court of the Settlement

Provision should be made for one of the parties to advise the court that a settlement has taken place, putting an end to the litigation file. The method of doing so varies depending on the jurisdiction where the settlement took place. For example, in Quebec, on behalf of their clients, the lawyers file a Declaration of Settlement out of court for the capital, interest, and costs, indicated in the lawsuit, once the terms and conditions of the agreement have been respected. In Ontario, on the other hand, the parties, by their respective lawyers file a Motion for an Order, on consent, dismissing the action without costs. Because of the differences that prevail across Canada, the settlement agreement should stipulate the procedure that is applicable in the jurisdiction in which the agreement was concluded.

### 12) Other Clauses

#### a) The Language of the Settlement Agreement

If the settlement agreement is in a language other than the official language of the jurisdiction in which the mediation was held, it should be stated that the parties expressly requested that the agreement be drafted in that language.

#### b) The Mediator's Fees and the Payment of Court Costs

The settlement agreement should include the payment of the mediator's fees and expenses, which are commonly shared by the parties. If the fees and expenses are not equally shared, the percentage payable by each party should be specified. Such a condition may have already been included in the mediator's mediation contract. However, if it has not already been included, then it should appear in the settlement agreement.

Another pertinent clause indicates who pays the court costs.

#### c) Severability

It may be necessary to specify that each provision and subsection of the settlement agreement is independent of the others and that if any provision or subsection is declared invalid or illegal by a competent court, the remaining provisions and subsections shall not be affected by such a declaration, but shall remain valid, binding, and enforceable.

#### d) The Parties' Declaration Regarding Comprehension, Assistance, and Satisfaction

Some agreements include a clause stating that the parties declare that they have read and understood the contents of the settlement agreement. Such a clause would also state that the parties have had the opportunity to obtain legal counsel and any other advice with respect to the scope of the agreement, that they expressly acknowledge that they agree with the terms and conditions of their settlement, which they consider to be reasonable, and that they are signing the settlement agreement freely and voluntarily, without duress of any kind.

#### e) The Names and Status of the Signatories

Finally, the settlement agreement should indicate the names of the signatories and their status. In the case of a corporation, a resolution of the board of directors, the basis for having the authorization to sign, or a mandate to act on behalf of a company or organization should be included. As for the lawyers, they should decide whether they sign the agreement as participants in the settlement.

### 13) Enforcement of the Settlement Agreement

It is wise to consider the enforcement of the settlement agreement. The manner of doing so varies from one province and territory to another. In Ontario, for example, the settlement agreement can include a draft judgment. If a party violates the terms or conditions of the agreement, the opposing party can present a motion to enforce the consent to judgment, which allows the enforcement of the agreement to take place more expeditiously.[2] In British Columbia, if an agreement is reached, the parties can ask the court for a consent order, containing the terms of the agreement. Once a judge signs the order, the agreement is enforceable by the court in the event that one of the parties fails to respect the agreement.[3] In Quebec, a similar procedure is available. Since the procedure is not the same across Canada, it is necessary to indicate the procedure that is applicable in the jurisdiction in which the agreement was concluded.

---

2 Natai Shelsen, "How to Enforce a Settlement Agreement" *Unsolicited Blog* (2023), online: https://goldblattpartners.com/alternative-dispute-resolution/mediation-alternative-dispute-resolution/how-to-enforce-a-settlement-agreement.

3 Government of British Columbia, "After Mediation," online: www2.gov.bc.ca/gov/content/justice/about-bcs-justice-system/mediation/about-mediation/after-mediation#:~:text=A%20consent%20order%20sets%20out,up%20to%20the%20settlement%20agreement.

## AN EXAMPLE OF A SETTLEMENT AGREEMENT

SETTLEMENT AGREEMENT entered into in the City and District of ____________ on May 1, 20___.[4]

**COURT OF ___________**
COUNTRY
PROVINCE
DISTRICT OF

No. X00-000-000000-000

BETWEEN JOHN SMITH, Residing and domiciled
At: 100 Main Street, in the City and District of
__________, Province of ____________
(Hereinafter referred to as Smith)

AND **FIXIT SERVICE INC**, a legal person having its head office located at 250 First Street, suite 5B, in the City and District of _________, Province of ___________
(Hereinafter referred to as Fixit)

**WHEREAS** on or about January ___, 20__, Smith instituted proceedings against Fixit before the Court of __________, bearing file number X00-000-000000-000 (the lawsuit), alleging unjust dismissal by the employer Fixit.

**WHEREAS** the parties, without admission of any kind on the part of either party, including any admission of liability, wish to terminate their lawsuit and settle their conflict by means of a Settlement Agreement, in accordance with the terms and conditions set out hereinafter.

**WHEREAS** the parties have agreed as follows:

4 This is an actual settlement agreement. However, the names of the parties and the undertakings set out in paragraph 2 are fictitious.

**1. The Preamble/Recital**

The Preamble (or the recital) forms an integral part of the present settlement agreement, as if recited at length, and serves to interpret its meaning and scope.

**2. Settlement Terms**

Fixit undertakes to pay Smith the sum of $________, less deductions at source, in three installments of equal amounts, on the following dates ____________ 20____, __________ 20____ , and __________ 20____.

The said amounts are payable by cheque, to the order of John Smith, and constitute the total amount payable in capital, interest, and costs.

Fixit undertakes to pay for outsourcing services to be given to Smith, by ABC Inc, for a total of $________, which is to be paid directly to ABC Inc, beginning on or before ________, 20____.

Fixit undertakes to transmit a letter of recommendation to Smith, on or before ________, 20____, the contents of which will be drafted jointly by the attorneys for both parties and approved by Smith.

Fixit also undertakes to assume the purchase of a computer for Smith for a maximum cost of $_______. This purchase shall be carried out on or before __________, 20____ , provided that Smith advises Fixit as to his choice of a computer at the latest on __________, 20____.

**3. Default**

If Fixit is in default of any of the above stated payments or any of its undertakings listed above, all sums shall become due and payable immediately together with the undertakings to transmit a letter of recommendation and purchase a computer.

**4. Receipt, Release, and Discharge**

In consideration of the obligations of Fixit cited above, Smith acknowledges the termination of the employment relationship with Fixit and renounces all recourses aimed at reinstatement.

In consideration of the present settlement agreement and the payment of the above cited sums, which represent full and final settlement of the present lawsuit, Smith hereby grants complete and final receipt, release, and discharge to Fixit and to its subsidiaries, affiliates, shareholders, directors, officers, managers, agents, employees, representatives, insurers, and/or successors of all actions, causes of action, lawsuits, debts, contracts, claims, demands, proceedings, damages, sums of money, and liabilities whatsoever, which Smith ever had, now has, or hereinafter can, shall or may have against Fixit, with respect to Smith's employment and/or to the termination of employment with Fixit and relating directly or indirectly to any and all allegations set out in the lawsuit.

### 5. Declaration of Settlement Out of Court

Smith undertakes to execute a Declaration of Settlement Out of Court[5] for the capital, interest, and costs with Fixit and provide copies of same to the legal counsel of Fixit, to be kept in trust.

Upon payment of the respective sums listed in paragraph 2 above and the execution of the above cited undertakings, the Declaration of Settlement Out of Court will be filed into the Court record in file number X00-000-000000-000 by Fixit's legal counsel.

### 6. General

The parties declare that the present settlement agreement was entered into to put an end to their lawsuit and to allow the parties to avoid further litigation and does not constitute an admission by either party of any duty, obligation, or wrongdoing of any nature whatsoever.

The parties declare and acknowledge that the present settlement agreement is the entire agreement between the parties with respect to the matters which are the subject of this settlement agreement and supersedes all previous agreements.

The parties declare that the present agreement constitutes a transaction[6] within the meaning of the law of Quebec and renounce any errors of fact, of law, and/or of calculation.

---

5 In Quebec, this term is used when a settlement puts an end to existing litigation. In the province of Ontario, a Consent is filed, consenting to the dismissal of the existing action.

6 In Quebec, a transaction is a contract by which the parties, by way of mutual concessions, prevent a future contestation, put an end to a lawsuit, or settle

The parties also declare and acknowledge that the present agreement was negotiated in good faith.

The parties expressly declare and acknowledge that they have read and understood the contents of this agreement. They declare that they had the opportunity to consult their respective counsel and have obtained legal counsel with respect to the scope and extent of the present agreement.

The parties also expressly acknowledge that the terms and conditions of the present agreement are reasonable and sufficient.

The parties declare that they signed the present agreement freely and voluntarily.

### 7. Governing Law and Forum

This agreement shall be governed by and interpreted in accordance with the laws of Quebec.

The ____________ Court of the Judicial District of __________ shall retain jurisdiction over the present matter until the conditions of the agreement have been met and it shall have exclusive jurisdiction with respect to any proceeding in connection with this agreement.

### 8. Severability

Each subsection and each provision of a subsection of this agreement is independent of the other, and if any subsection or provision of the agreement is declared invalid, illegal, or unenforceable by final judgment of a competent Court, then the remaining subsections and provisions shall not be affected by such a declaration and shall remain valid, binding, and enforceable.

### 9. Binding effect

This agreement shall be binding upon and inure to the benefit of the parties hereto and their respective successors, and legal representatives, and shall not be assignable or transferable.

---

difficulties that arise in the execution of a judgment. The document is generally referred as an agreement, a settlement, or a transaction. In the common law provinces, such an agreement would simply be referred to as a settlement agreement or a binding agreement.

### 10. Confidentiality

The present agreement and its contents are confidential. The parties undertake not to reveal, remit, or otherwise divulge to any third party the present agreement and its contents, either verbally or in writing, except if required to do so by law or to their respective advisors if needed for financial and/or legal advice, and excepting any enforcement authorities.

### 11. Costs

Each party shall pay their own costs.

### 12. Language

The parties acknowledge that they have required and consented that this agreement and all related documents be prepared in English. Les parties reconnaissent avoir exigé que la présente convention et tous les documents connexes soient rédigés en anglais.[7]

**AND THE PARTIES HAVE SIGNED:**

In the City of ________________ District of ____________________

_________________________ ______________________________

Plaintiff Defendant

7 This addition is used in agreements where French is the official language of the jurisdiction in which the settlement takes place.

## B. A PARTIAL AGREEMENT IS REACHED

If the parties settle some of the issues without putting an end to the conflict, an agreement can nevertheless be concluded dealing with those items agreed upon and the issues that were resolved. If a lawsuit has already been instituted, it can then be limited to the unresolved issues or, alternatively, the parties can agree to another means of resolving the remaining aspects of their conflict.

Where an agreement has been reached, whether it is complete or partial, parties tend to be satisfied with the process. Their satisfaction stems from their ability to arrive at an outcome that may be creative, that solves their conflict, and that takes into consideration their emotional state.

## C. NO AGREEMENT IS REACHED

If your clients do not settle at the end of a mediation session, do not be discouraged. Parties participating in mediation do not always settle their conflict. They are not required to do so. Even in jurisdictions where mediation is mandatory, the parties must attend a mediation session, but there is no obligation for them to come to an agreement.

In court mandated mediations, the judge/mediator prepares a report indicating whether or not the parties have settled their dispute. The lack of settlement should not be referred to as a *failure*. Rather, the fact that the parties did not resolve their conflict simply means that the final proposals on the table did not meet their interests and needs. The parties ultimately preferred to have a decision rendered by the court, which they considered to be a better alternative to a settlement they considered unsatisfactory.

In instances where no settlement is reached, the parties proceed to trial. If they have participated in a settlement conference presided over by a judge, the trial will be presided over by a different judge who was not involved in the settlement discussions. As already indicated, when parties have participated in a mediation or a settlement conference, their discussions, documents, offers, and concessions remain confidential and, except for exceptional circumstances, cannot be disclosed in a trial.

## D. ENFORCEMENT OF THE AGREEMENT

Parties settle their conflict by working together and finding an acceptable solution. Since any agreement concluded in mediation must be acceptable to both parties, the level of compliance with a mediated settlement is generally very high. There are nevertheless several reasons why parties subsequently may no longer respect their agreement. One or the other party may change their mind, regretting having accepted the final proposal. A change in an organization's leadership or business losses may lead to a failure to comply. Often, the reason stems from a misunderstanding between the parties as to the exact terms and conditions they had agreed upon.

If one of the parties breaches the terms of the agreement, the other party can take steps to have the agreement enforced by the court. The procedure varies from one province and territory to another. Furthermore, in some provinces, enforcement of the agreement can be obtained only after a breach in compliance has occurred, while in other provinces, proceedings can be undertaken as a precaution before a breach even occurs,[8] so that if a party fails to respect the agreement, the enforcement can immediately take place. The courts generally do not examine the merits or the appropriateness of an agreement. Their role is limited to examining whether an agreement had, in fact, been reached by the parties.

For the court to conclude that there was indeed an agreement putting an end to the parties' conflict and constituting a binding agreement, there must be evidence of unconditional acceptance of an outstanding offer between the parties. Most importantly, the parties must have agreed on all the essential elements relating to the agreement.

---

8 Thomas Neeser, "Verjee Law: Deal or No Deal — Keys to Enforcing a Settlement Agreement" Verjee Law (2023), online: https://verjee-law.com/verjee-law-deal-or-no-deal-keys-to-enforcing-a-settlement-agreement/.

The essential terms of the agreement must possess a sufficient degree of clarity for it to be legally binding. If the agreement is incomplete or too general, a binding agreement will not have been created. The purported agreement, in such a case, may be characterized as *an agreement to agree*;[9] however, it is not enforceable. It is therefore essential that the terms agreed upon be clear and concise. The failure of the parties to agree on the essential terms of their agreement will prevent the creation of a binding contract.

Therefore, it is extremely important when drafting the content of an agreement that both parties have the same understanding of the terms. Since settlements are encouraged by our justice system, Canadian courts will strive to give effect to the parties' intentions. Accordingly, once an agreement shows the unambiguous intention of the parties to settle their conflict and create a legal relationship, the courts will interpret the agreement such that it will be rendered enforceable.

There are nevertheless circumstances where the courts will not enforce a settlement. The courts have discretion to refuse to enforce settlement agreements that are unconscionable.[10] Examples of such agreements involve settlements that are grossly unfair to one of the parties, where one of the parties failed to receive independent legal advice, where there is a power imbalance that is overwhelming, and where parties have taken advantage of a vulnerable party.[11]

## E. FINAL COMMENTS

As stated above, parties do not always settle their conflict. It is important to remember that when parties do not settle, there may still be a possibility for them to reach an agreement later. Some mediators keep the file open for a certain time and reconvene the

9 Daniel Waldman, "A Settlement Agreement Is a Binding Contract. Not an 'Agreement to Agree'" Pallett Valo LLP (5 November 2019), online: www.pallettvalo.com/whats-trending/a-settlement-agreement-is-a-binding-contract-not-an-agreement-to-agree/.

10 *Huma v Mississauga Hospital*, 2020 ONCA 644 at para 25.

11 Shelsen, above note 2.

parties to see if any agreement can be reached after the mediation session has ended. Nothing prevents you from discussing the last option or offers put on the table with your clients after the mediation session is over to determine whether they are more amenable to settling.

If your clients are open either to accepting the final offer from the opposite party or to continuing the discussions, with the consent of the other party and their counsel, you can contact the mediator to see whether another mediation session can be held. Alternatively, you can attempt to resolve the conflict without the mediator by contacting the opposing lawyer and continuing to discuss settlement options with the parties. Experience has shown that the discussions and negotiations that take place in a mediation session often provide the basis for a later settlement.

However, even in cases where the parties do not reach an agreement, the mediation process is not a useless exercise. The feedback from those who have participated in mediations is incredibly positive. Mediation enables the parties involved to have a better understanding of the other party's perspective, which can decrease their hostility toward each other. The mediation also provides the parties with an opportunity to experience a process which, rather than being adversarial and hostile, seeks to find a positive means of resolving differences.

❋ ❋ ❋ ❋ ❋

Although it is a fact that some cases do not result in an agreement, most cases do settle. The changed legal culture, the satisfaction of the parties who participate in mediations, and your knowledge of how to effectively represent your clients in mediation should provide you with the incentive to recommend this dispute resolution method to your clients.

Why litigate when you can mediate? Hopefully, mediation is the path you will recommend to your clients.

*appendix one*

# Reminders for the Mediation

Although the main aspects of the topics to be discussed with your clients have been covered in the text, the following are a few reminders as to what you should do and what you should say to your clients before attending a mediation session, as well as how to handle the mediation itself.

## A. HOW TO PREPARE YOUR CLIENTS

Review the facts of the case with your clients and prepare a checklist of the events that took place in chronological order so that it will be easy for them to present their version of the story without memorizing any part of it.

Similarly, ask them to list their emotions and how they were impacted by the opposing party's words and behaviour. Do a mock presentation with your clients and point out potential pitfalls.

In the same way that you would do a rehearsal for a trial, which includes a cross-examination of your own clients to see how they will do in court, before the mediation takes place, play the role of the opposite party. You could object to what your clients say, shake your head, call them names, shout at them, or react negatively to their presentation and proposals, to make sure that your clients will behave appropriately to any provocation on the part of the other party when they are in the mediation session.

Review the items discussed in Chapter 4, dealing with the preparation for mediation.

Do not forget to find out what your clients' interests and needs are, as well as those of the opposite party. They are always a key element in reaching an agreement.

Finally, advise your clients to dress appropriately for the mediation. Although the process is far less formal than in court, it is not appropriate to attend the mediation session in jeans and a T-shirt.

## B. WHAT TO TELL YOUR CLIENTS

It is important to emphasize when talking to your clients that they will not be attending the mediation to win their case. Neither side will get everything they want. There will be a give and take, and, ultimately, there will have to be some compromise if your clients want to settle. The goal is for both parties to obtain a solution that is sufficiently acceptable so that they can end their conflict. Going to court is always a risk.

Explain the roles of each participant. Remind your clients that the mediator will be controlling the mediation, but the mediator will not be rendering a decision, determining the outcome of the conflict, or ordering the content of any agreement that may be reached. That is the role of the parties.

Remind your clients that you will be taking a back seat in the process but assure them that you will be continually available to assist and advise them. Your role is to collaborate in trying to help your clients find a satisfactory solution.

Describe the mediation as a step-by-step process. After the mediator's introduction, each party presents their facts of the case. Make sure that your clients are prepared to express their version of the case in a clear and chronological order. When the negotiations begin, one party must start by presenting the first proposal. Often, your clients will be reticent to begin, wanting to hear what the other party puts on the table.

If your clients are the plaintiffs, in most instances, they will be the ones expected to present the first proposal. However, they should not be concerned. Because this is a topic that you have discussed with them, they should be ready to begin. If your clients are the defendants, they can request that the plaintiffs go first. However, you should nevertheless prepare your clients to make a reasonable offer if the plaintiffs decline to indicate what they are seeking.

Talk to your clients about the caucus, what its purpose is, and how it can be used. Encourage them to tell you when they want to talk to you and the mediator in private, in which case you will ask the mediator to hold a caucus. Similarly, if they want to talk to you privately, they should feel free to ask for a break to be able to meet with you alone.

Tell your clients that the mediator may ask to have a caucus first with the other party. This does not show favouritism. It does not matter which party the mediator meets with first. Most often, mediators will meet in caucus with each party, one at a time.

There are no set rules for the negotiating process. There are nevertheless strategies to be adopted that will be useful in obtaining a good settlement. The negotiations involve back-and-forth discussions between the parties. Underline the need to listen to the opposite party and be open to new options. Instead of dwelling on what caused the conflict, tell your clients to concentrate on how to go forward. Ask them to articulate what a good agreement will be for them. Then review with your clients the means of persuading the opposing party to accept such an agreement.

Advise your clients not to begin with an extreme position, but with a reasonable one. Have your clients think about solutions that will be satisfactory not only for them but for the other party as well.

If the other party is challenging a proposal provided by your clients, instead of defending it, tell your clients to explain it to the other party. Instead of debating what the other party wants, suggest that your clients ask questions, talk about fairness, look at factors that can be used as objective standards, such as the market price, the average cost of rebuilding or replacing, the depreciation of the item, and so on. It can be a good approach to suggest that both parties obtain several quotes to review or seek the input of a third party.

Urge your clients to be creative and to think about any non-monetary options that they could propose. Such options, like an exchange or the provision of services or the purchase of equipment, may be advantageous for both parties, since it may be of interest or beneficial to the plaintiffs and less costly for the defendants.

Try to determine how comfortable your clients are about the pace of the negotiations. Do they want to reach an outcome quickly, or would they prefer getting there slowly? Even if they have an idea as to how fast they want to get to their bottom line, explain that they should see how the opposing party negotiates. This will allow them to reconsider whether or not they should move toward their bottom line quickly.

When negotiating, be mindful of the amounts put on the table. If your clients are the defendants, proposing smaller and smaller increases in the amount they are willing to pay will signal that they are near their bottom line. Similarly, if your clients are the plaintiffs, proposing smaller and smaller decreases in the amount they will accept will indicate that they are reaching their bottom line.

To determine what an appropriate settlement can be, in cases where the issue is solely money, discuss with your clients what the outcome may be if the case goes to trial. Point out that in determining what amount they will potentially receive as plaintiffs or what they might have to pay if they are the defendants, they must consider court costs, the amount of interest to be paid, your fees, the fees of an expert, if one is needed, and the cost of the time they will not be able to spend at their business, profession, or work.

Once the net amount is calculated, your clients will have a more realistic idea of what they may expect in a judgment. This is the basis on which to decide whether going to court is the Best Alternative to a Negotiated Agreement (BATNA). Your clients will want to have an agreement that is better than going to court.

Then determine with your clients what their bottom line is, that is, the point at which they will be prepared to go to trial rather than accept the final proposal on the table. Given that parties must compromise in mediations, your calculations and discussions can help your clients understand, before they go to the mediation, what it will take for them to reach an agreement. In addition, remind your clients that there are always risks involved in going to court. In addition, there will be delays, stress, and uncertainties.

Even if the only issue in the conflict is money, there may nevertheless be modalities that can be negotiated, which can sweeten the deal. Examples of such modalities include a lesser amount of interest payable, the payment of the money in instalments, and the amount of each instalment payment. These options should also be discussed before the mediation session.

Remind your clients they should not settle too quickly since there should be some back-and-forth discussion of the proposals, between the parties, before an agreement is reached.

Finally, tell your clients to listen to their opponent, try to understand their view, consider their interests, and encourage your clients to be optimistic and positive about coming to an agreement.

*appendix two*

# Useful Tips—Dos and Don'ts

Some behaviour enhances the possibility of settling, while other actions are counterproductive. Several "dos and don'ts" have already been included in the text. The following are suggestions that may be given to your clients to help them improve their negotiations:

1) Listen to what the other party says. If you show that you are listening to the opposing party, there is more likelihood that party will listen to your version of events.
2) Be positive. Express your confidence that both parties will find a way to settle the conflict.
3) Tell the opposite party that you appreciate their willingness to participate in the mediation.
4) Show empathy for the other party's feelings.
5) Use reframing techniques. Try whenever possible to turn a negative comment from the other party into a positive one. At the very least, turn it into a neutral statement.
6) Rather than blame the other party for what was done or said, tell the other party what the impact the words or actions had on you. The opposing party will be far more understanding if you say, *We feel* . . . or *We felt* . . . rather than saying *You did* . . . .
7) Show understanding. Even when you do not agree with a statement made by the opposite party, rather than saying they are wrong, it is more productive to say that you understand, although you are not in agreement. Similarly, when you do

not accept a proposal put forward by the other party, rather than saying that the proposal is unacceptable, state that it is an interesting proposition, but suggest other possibilities.

8) Be open minded. The other party may present proposals that you had not considered which could be potential solutions.
9) Remain calm. When the other party is angry or lashes out, it is important to reduce the level of emotion. No solution is achieved in anger.
10) Collaborate as much as possible. Engage the other party to brainstorm with you to find solutions that are satisfactory to both parties.
11) Don't give up. Breakthroughs can take place at the final hour. As long as both parties are still present and talking to each other, concluding in an agreement remains possible.

The approach that works best is to be positive and collaborative. Conversely, confrontational behaviour or statements should be avoided. The following are examples of what not to do or say:

1) Do not act in a condescending or arrogant manner toward the other party. It will not endear you to the other party. Rather, that party may feel inadequate or intimidated by you.
2) Do not ridicule or humiliate the other party. Belittling your opponent will do nothing to advance your case.
3) Do not attack the credibility of the other party. This will also do nothing to advance your case.
4) Do not be rude. Such negativity only produces the same behaviour in the other party.
5) Do not raise your voice or scream at the other party. The other party may respond in kind.
6) Do not use inflammatory language or provoke the other party, such as accusing your opponent of lying or misrepresenting the facts. No one likes being called a liar or any other names.
7) Do not threaten the other party. It may induce your opponent to leave.

8) Do not make faces or roll your eyes when the other party is speaking. Your body language indicates that you think that what the other party is saying is preposterous.
9) Do not criticize proposals made by the opposite party.
10) Avoid using absolutes when discussing proposals. Expressions such as *over my dead body*, *out of the question*, *never*, or *impossible* are not very productive.

*appendix three*

# Summary and Checklist

The following is a list of the elements involved in the mediation process from the outset—when you propose mediation as a means of resolving the conflict—to the end of the mediation session.

## A. INTRODUCTION

Explain the various means of settling conflict to your clients, including the differences between the various methods. Talk to your clients about the nature of mediation and your role in the process.

## B. INITIATING THE MEDIATION PROCESS

### 1) Discuss, with your clients, the possibility of choosing mediation to resolve their conflict

Explain to your clients what mediation entails. Suggest that they participate in mediation (or in a settlement conference) rather than go to court to resolve their case. In your attempt to convince them, list the many advantages of mediation when compared with litigation:

- The possibility of selecting an appropriate mediator.
- The rapidity of scheduling a mediation session.
- The lack of formality.
- The flexibility of the process.
- The opportunity to express feelings or emotions.
- The fact that the process is less costly than a trial.

- The fact that the process is less stressful than a trial.
- The fact that the process is less time consuming than a trial.
- The fact that the mediation is confidential.
- The possibility of determining the issues to be discussed.
- The possibility of resolving issues that go beyond the subject matter of a lawsuit.
- The possibility of speaking directly to the other party.
- The opportunity to explain one's perspective on the conflict.
- The possibility of re-establishing, maintaining, continuing, or improving a relationship.
- Better input in the process and better control over the results than a trial.
- The opportunity to be creative and find imaginative solutions.
- The avoidance of a potentially unfavourable judgment.
- The possibility that a settlement will be advantageous for third parties who are impacted by the conflict.
- The possibility of finding a solution that a judge cannot order.
- The involvement of your clients in finding a satisfactory solution adapted to their interests and needs.
- The immediate knowledge of the outcome.
- Likelihood of better compliance with the settlement.
- Most importantly, a solution that is *made to measure*.

**2) Propose mediation to the opposite party or lawyer**

Contact the opposing party or the opposing party's lawyer to suggest settling the conflict by mediation. Alternatively, present a mediation proposal in your demand letter. This could include, for example:

Under reserve of our claim against you, and in order to resolve this dispute quickly and in an amicable manner, we are authorized to advise you that our clients are open to settlement discussions. Accordingly, if such an approach is acceptable to you and, if you agree to participate in a mediation, please advise the undersigned on or before (the date) and we will contact you to begin the process of selecting a mediator, a location, and a date for the mediation.

### 3) Respond to a demand letter sent to your clients

If a demand letter your clients have received does not contain a proposal to mediate, it is nevertheless an option to answer the demand with your own mediation proposal:

Consequently, as indicated above, our clients deny all responsibility with respect to your allegations and will vigorously contest any legal proceedings that are instituted.

However, under reserve of our denial of responsibility and our vigorous contestation, I wish to advise you that our clients have authorized us to explore with you the possibility of participating in a mediation session, with the aim of settling this dispute rapidly. If you are interested in this approach as a means of reaching an amiable solution, you can contact the undersigned on or before (the date) to discuss the manner of proceeding, including the selection of a mediator, the timing, and location of the mediation session.

### 4) Select a mediator

In selecting a mediator for your mediation, consider the mediator's:

- training and certification,
- approach,
- style,
- attributes,
- expertise,
- availability,
- cost,
- reputation, and
- lack of any conflict of interest with respect to you or your clients.

There are several questions to consider in selecting an appropriate mediator:

- Do you want a mediator whose approach is that of classical mediation, or do you want an evaluative mediator?
- What type of personality and personal attributes of the mediator correspond best with your clients' personalities?

- Do you need someone with specialized knowledge or expertise, or is a generalist sufficient?
- How quickly do you need to schedule the mediation and resolve the conflict?
- How much can your clients afford to pay for the mediation?
- Is there any conflict of interest between the mediator you want to hire and either you or your clients?

Select a mediator whose profile meets your clients' needs.

**5) Determine the location of the mediation, if it will not be held virtually**

Consider the following aspects:

- a location that is neutral or comfortable for your clients,
- sufficient space for all participants,
- separate, acoustically isolated rooms for caucuses,
- the availability of flip charts or blackboards,
- the availability of washrooms nearby,
- accessible parking facilities or transportation, and
- lunch arrangements or the existence of restaurants nearby.

**6) Determine the details of a virtual mediation session**

In the case of virtual mediation sessions, there are several other considerations to keep in mind:

- Ensure that you and your clients are familiar with the platform to be used, and if your clients are uncomfortable, ask that the mediation be held in person.
- Determine when the link will be provided and ensure that a link has been sent.
- Verify that your equipment is in good working order and that you have good sound and lighting.
- Inquire whether the mediator uses breakout rooms for caucusing.
- Ensure there will be no disturbances during the mediation.
- Tell your clients to wear appropriate clothing at the mediation session.

- Advise your clients not to multi-task during the mediation session and to turn off their cellphones.
- Ensure that the camera on your computer is in a good position and that you and your clients can easily be seen.
- Ensure that your background is appropriate.
- Ensure that you have technical support available if necessary and determine whether other options are foreseen if the parties become disconnected with each other or with the mediator.
- Advise your clients to turn off their microphone during any breaks.
- Ask that the time be limited to a few hours or half a day and that if more time is needed, another date be scheduled.
- If a conclusion is not reached by the time the mediation session is terminated, ensure that another date has been chosen.
- Ensure that you or you clients have a scanner to send and receive documents.
- Obtain a copy of the agreement signed by both parties, if a settlement is reached.

**7) Schedule the mediation session**

Considerations to keep in mind if you foresee that the mediation will take more than one day to conclude:

- Schedule more than one meeting at the outset.
- Request that the dates be set close to each other.
- Ensure the availability of your clients and any other participants.

**8) Draft the mediation contract**

Important elements to consider:

- Review the provisions of the contact.
- Ensure the usual clauses are included.
- Discuss the contents with your clients.
- Ensure that the mandate given to the mediator is clear.
- Ensure that the date(s) of the mediation session(s), the date the documents and/or exhibits must be remitted, the fees, and costs of the mediator are specified.

- Ensure that each party's share of the mediator's fees and expenses is specified.
- Ensure that you have the right to end the mediation, if needed.
- Ensure that your clients accept the terms of the contract.

### 9) Draft the confidentiality agreement

Review the terms of the confidentiality agreement:

- Explain the reason for the confidentiality of all communication between parties in order to settle a conflict.
- Determine whether there is an option to obtain legal or financial advice.
- Explain the nature of the agreement and the limitations of confidentiality clauses to your clients.
- Ensure that your clients understand the importance of respecting this agreement.

## C. THE INTERESTS AND NEEDS OF THE PARTIES

Question your clients to determine whether any of the following interests and/or needs are applicable in their case and whether there are any other considerations that are important to them as a means of settling the conflict:

- maintaining their reputations
- preserving the confidentiality of the conflict
- avoiding public embarrassment
- avoiding the creation of a precedent for future cases
- being heard and understood
- obtaining an explanation from the opposing party
- obtaining acknowledgement or respect from the other party
- obtaining an apology or expression of regret
- re-establishing a relationship
- establishing future business relations
- ending the conflict quickly
- obtaining financial compensation

Note any interests or needs that your clients should raise at the mediation session.

## D. PREPARING FOR MEDIATION

Use a checklist to ensure that all steps that can be taken before the mediation have been taken:

- Prepare your clients for the mediation session.
- Describe the nature and the objectives of the mediation process to your clients.
- Describe the usual steps of the mediation process.
- Describe the role of the mediator, the parties, and the lawyers.
- Describe what will take place at the mediation session.
- Discuss how to dress for the mediation session.
- Determine who will take part in the mediation session:
  - ▹ the party to the proceedings.
  - ▹ the person aware of the facts.
  - ▹ the person with the authority to settle.
  - ▹ the expert witness, if needed and if the mediator agrees, and
  - ▹ an insurance representative, if your client is represented by an insurance company.
- Determine whether any language barriers exist.
  - ▹ If so, consider hiring an interpreter and advise the mediator of this necessity.
- Determine whether any cultural issues exist.
  - ▹ If so, raise the differences in the mediation session to explain how the conflict arose.
- Discuss and list the strengths and weaknesses of your clients' case and the strengths and weaknesses of the other party.
  - ▹ The strengths of your client's case can be used as a negotiating tool.
  - ▹ The weaknesses of your client's case can be used to encourage them to modify their position.
- Identify and list the interests and needs of both parties.

- Prepare the documents and facts that may be needed at the mediation session.
- Prepare a brief for the mediator, if such a brief has been requested.
  - ▹ If so, determine the contents required.
- Prepare your clients to present their version of the facts of the case.
  - ▹ Create a checklist with them, containing the events in chronological order, to jog their memory and facilitate their presentation
- Prepare your clients to discuss their emotions.
  - ▹ List the emotions and feelings they will present.
- Do a mock presentation with them.
- Discuss the amount your clients are willing to offer or to accept at the outset.
- Think outside the box and consider non-monetary proposals.
  - ▹ If such possibilities exist, list them for easy reference.
- Discuss strategy with your clients, including:
  - ▹ any non-starter issues that will prevent the mediation from taking place,
  - ▹ the order of subjects to be discussed,
  - ▹ the use of caucuses and when they should request a caucus, and
  - ▹ the pace of the negotiations and whether your clients are comfortable moving quickly or slowly towards a settlement.
- Determine your clients' bottom line
- Discuss your clients' BATNA and their best-case and worst-case scenarios.
- Discuss the costs involved in not reaching a settlement.

## E. THE MEDIATION PROCESS

### 1) The Opening by the Mediator

- Seat your clients close to the mediator and, if possible, facing the opposite party.

### 2) The Presentation of the Facts

- Ensure that your clients have their checklist, so that they will be able to tell their version of the facts in a chronological and coherent manner.
- Ensure that they have a list of dos and don'ts. Advise them to:
  - ▹ talk directly to the opposite party,
  - ▹ set out their facts in a chronological order,
  - ▹ detail the incident that led to the conflict,
  - ▹ express their feelings and the impact that the opposite party's words and behaviour had on them,
  - ▹ avoid legal jargon,
  - ▹ avoid insults, threats, and condescending language, and
  - ▹ be respectful and sympathetic and indicate their appreciation to the opposite party for agreeing to participate in the mediation.
- Ask your clients questions if they forget or omit important details.
- Listen actively to the opposite party to better understand that party's position, strengths, and weaknesses.
- Note non-verbal communication.

### 3) The Interests and Needs of your Clients

- Have your clients express their interests and needs when they present their version of the facts.
- Listen carefully to the version of the opposite party to determine their interests and needs.

### 4) The Negotiation and Selection of Options for Settlement

Your approach should be that of collaborative negotiation, not positional negotiations. Make sure to:

- Present constructive comments.
- Determine the issues to be resolved.
- Determine the order of the issues to be discussed.
- Present a first proposal that is reasonable and credible.
- Present several proposals, if possible.
- Leave more difficult issues to resolve to the end.

- React to unacceptable proposals of the other side without hostility; instead, ask questions, reframe statements, and seek collaboration.
- Determine who is deciding on the other side and who must be involved in order to settle successfully.
  - ▷ Meet separately with the other party's lawyer when that party is not cooperating, or arrange for a meeting of the parties alone.
- Note the style of the other party. Do what is necessary to accommodate your clients.
- Do not try to settle too quickly. There should be at least one refusal from both your clients and the other party before a settlement is reached.
- Keep close tabs on the pace of the negotiations. Ensure that your clients are not pressured by the other party's rapid pace. If your clients' pace is to move quickly, ensure that they do not rapidly concede too much.
- Consider the interests and needs of the opposite party. Try to determine how they can be addressed when presenting proposals to induce that party to settle.
- Advise the mediator when you wish to caucus.
- Ask for a caucus to:
  - ▷ present an offer,
  - ▷ consider a proposal from the other party,
  - ▷ allow your clients to let off steam,
  - ▷ allow your clients to regain composure,
  - ▷ deal with aggressive behaviour,
  - ▷ deal with intimidating behaviour or threats from the other party,
  - ▷ be open with the mediator,
  - ▷ obtain clarification of an issue that has been discussed,
  - ▷ obtain information from the mediator concerning what would induce the opposing party to settle,
  - ▷ consider alternative proposals, or to raise new ideas,
  - ▷ do a reality check with your clients,
  - ▷ reassess your clients' position, considering the new information that has been presented,

  - ▹ encourage your clients to modify their position if that is needed,
  - ▹ discuss with your clients the risks of not settling and going to trial,
  - ▹ discuss your clients' concerns,
  - ▹ discuss the benefits of settling,
  - ▹ re-evaluate your negotiation strategy,
  - ▹ provide the mediator with your clients' offers or position,
  - ▹ provide the mediator with your clients' bottom line, or
  - ▹ speak confidentially with the mediator about any other matter.
- Consider means of breaking impasses or deadlocks by using some of the same techniques as the mediator, such as:
  - ▹ Ask for a caucus in which you will ask the mediator to provide an opinion on the strengths and weaknesses of your clients' case and to convey your clients' strengths to the opposite party.
  - ▹ Contact a third party to obtain further information.
  - ▹ Raise possible propositions and ask questions.
  - ▹ Meet with the other lawyer to obtain assistance in brainstorming and in trying to find a solution for both parties.
  - ▹ Request that the parties meet by themselves if the opposing lawyer is counterproductive and where the parties have a long-standing relationship with each other.
  - ▹ Take a break from the mediation session.
  - ▹ Talk about the costs and risks of going to trial.
  - ▹ Talk about the best- and worst-case scenarios if the parties go to trial.
  - ▹ Ask the parties to consider another issue.
  - ▹ Brainstorm, think outside the box, and consider alternate proposals and creative proposals that are beneficial for the plaintiffs and not costly for the defendants.
- Use strategies to persuade the opposite party, such as:
  - ▹ Inform the other party that your clients have a better alternative to a negotiated settlement.
  - ▹ Talk about common interests.
  - ▹ Refer to established criteria and comparable cases.

   - ▷ Make a firm offer that is available for a limited period of time.
- Consider proposals.
   - ▷ When possible options are presented, discuss them further, but in the case of an unacceptable proposal, present a counter proposal.
   - ▷ Suggest various proposals and use a process of elimination to find an acceptable option or options.
- When it comes to the final offer, determine whether it is appropriate for your clients to accept the proposal or whether it is better to go to court.
- When advising your clients to settle:
   - ▷ determine whether the other party's best proposal is as good or better than the best outcome your clients can obtain from court,
   - ▷ ensure that your clients' interests and needs are met,
   - ▷ ensure that your clients are satisfied with the outcome, and
   - ▷ ensure that your clients' legal interests have been protected.

## F. THE CONCLUSION

### 1) When an Agreement Is Reached

The agreement should include the following information:

1) All the terms and conditions in clear, plain language.
2) The parties to the agreement.
3) The preamble or the recitals, including a description of the claim and an affirmation of the voluntary nature of the agreement concluded by the parties.
4) The absence of liability.
5) The compensation or consideration:
   a) If the agreement entails a sum of money, indicate:
      - Who will be paying the amount of money agreed upon?
      - What is the amount payable?
      - What is the currency?
      - Will the money be paid in a lump sum or in instalments?
      - What is the date or dates on which it will be payable?

- In the case of instalment payments, what is the frequency of the payments and how much is payable in each instalment?
- Will any interest or penalty be foreseen for late payments?
- If interest is foreseen, what percentage will it be?
- How will payment be made: by cheque, a money order, an e-transfer, or cash?
- Will payment go to the clients or to their lawyer in trust?
- Where will the payment be made? Will it be made at the plaintiffs' personal address, their business address, or their lawyer's office, or transferred directly to their bank account?
- Are there any tax consequences?

b) If the agreement involves an alternate means of payment, indicate the specifics. If a service is to be provided:
- What is the nature of the service?
- Who will be providing the service?
- When will the service be provided?
- If it takes place on more than one occasion, on what dates will it be provided?
- If a third party is involved, what are the details of the involvement and the coordinates of that party?

c) If goods are to be provided, include:
- a complete description of the goods and of the supplier or vendor,
- the date or dates on which they will be provided,
- whether a warranty is required for the goods
- what the warranty will cover,
- how long the warranty will apply, and
- the length of time parts will be available.

d) If a letter of recommendation is involved, include:
- who will be drafting the letter,
- what the letter will contain, and
- a note that the contents of the letter must be approved.

e) If an apology is involved:
- the content of the apology must be determined.

6) The binding effect of the agreement.

7) The confidentiality of the agreement, any exceptions, and the applicable penalty if confidentiality is not respected.
8) The law and jurisdiction governing the agreement.
9) The release.
10) The sanctions that will apply if either party fails to respect their agreement.
11) Details about who will advise the court that the parties have reached a settlement once the terms and conditions of the agreement have been met.
12) Other clauses:
    - the language of the agreement,
    - the payment of the mediator's fees and court costs,
    - severability,
    - the parties' declaration regarding assistance and their satisfaction, and
    - the names and status of the signatories.
13) Details about how the agreement will be enforced.

### 2) When a Partial Agreement Is Reached

Prepare the content of the agreement reached in the same way as when the entire conflict has been settled. The remaining items that were not settled will be the object of either an alternate means of settling or a court case.

### 3) When No Agreement Is Reached

Express your appreciation to the other party for participating in the mediation and for attempting to reach an agreement.

Tell the other party that although you did not settle the conflict, you are open to continuing discussions at another time, prior to the trial date, and you hope that you can reach an agreement in the future. Alternatively ask the mediator if another mediation session can be scheduled.

### 4) Enforcement of the Agreement

If a breach of the agreement occurs, take steps to have the agreement enforced.

# Index

## ABOUT THE AUTHOR

**Suzanne Handman** obtained a law degree from the University of Montreal after an initial career as a clinician and Associate Professor in Speech Therapy and Audiology. She joined the firm of Trudel, Nadeau and associates and subsequently became a partner.

In 1994, She was appointed a Vice Chair of the Canada Labour Relations Board (now the Canada Industrial Relations Board) and in 2000, she was appointed Judge of the Quebec Labour Tribunal. In 2005, she transferred to the Civil Division of the Court of Quebec.

During her career on the bench, she began a mediation program at the Quebec Labour Tribunal. At the Court of Quebec, in addition to presiding over trials, she was very active conducting settlement conferences.

Now retired, Suzanne Handman continues to mediate conflicts. She is on the Board of Directors of the International Mediation Council and regularly teaches mediation skills. She has authored several articles on dispute resolution and has given presentations in Montreal and in France on the subject of mediation.

Suzanne Handman is married to Bjørn U. Ellingsen and lives in Montreal.

Printed and bound by CPI Group (UK) Ltd, Croydon, CR0 4YY
15/09/2026
14962401-0002